LAID BARE

About the Author

Tom Judson has written music and lyrics for film, television and the theater. He has acted both on and off-Broadway and on various stages throughout the world. His writing has appeared on numerous websites and blogs and in many different magazines and newspapers. For his work in gay adult films (as "Gus Mattox") he was awarded the GayVN Performer of the Year Award and is, as of this writing, the oldest recipient of that honor.

LAID BARE

Essays and Observations

Tom Judson

Cover photograph by John Skalicky
Cover design by Tom Judson
Interior design by Johnathan Wilber

Earlier versions of these essays have appeared in *Unzipped Magazine, Equity News, Blue Magazine,* as well as on various websites and blogs.

for Irwin and Arlene

CONTENTS

Introduction

My husband, Bruce, loved American popular music. Coming of age in the late 1970s he was particularly fond of the more esoteric sounds of that era: artists like Bryan Ferry, The New York Dolls and—especially—Patti Smith. His tastes weren't limited to the current scene, though; he also listened to the Phil Spector catalog and early Beatles. But his favorite records were the R&B singles from Motown. He knew all the great vocal groups coming out of Detroit in the '60s and '70s.

And that's because he always wanted to be a backup singer. Specifically, Bruce wanted to be a Pip. An unlikely ambition for a skinny Jewish guy from Scarsdale, perhaps, but Bruce was convinced that the Pips had the best backup arrangements going. Especially on "Midnight Train to Georgia".

It's worth noting that Bruce didn't want to be the star. The Pips were not in the spotlight, but they were essential. Being a Pip seemed to me to be the goal of someone who was comfortable with his place in the world. I was the hambone actor/composer in the family, but Bruce truly relished his role as the supportive spouse who rushes to the stage at the end of the performance with a huge bouquet of flowers.

When he would talk about The Pips, though, things were different. He took center stage in any discussion of their records. Bruce's demeanor could best be described as "animated" *(He's fucking hyper!* his father would say.) While I sat in a chair listening to the backing vocal of "Midnight Train to Georgia" Bruce would stand in front of me like a boxer in the ring, dancing his weight from one foot to the other, waiting to see my reaction to the song. He was right: The Pips *rock* on this record. Their backup almost stands on its own as a parallel song to Gladys Knight's lead. *"A superstar, but he didn't get far..."* *"It's his and hers alone..."* *"I know you will..."* These aren't echoes of the song—they're separate, independent lyric phrases that form a counterpoint to the main tune.

In his quest to become a Pip, Bruce would put on his red satin dinner jacket and play the 45 R.P.M. of "Midnight Train to Georgia" over and over while improvising Soul Train choreography in our living room. His enthusiasm may have outweighed his talent, but he gave it one hundred percent and would beam like a kid when the needle lifted out of the groove at the end of the record.

Life with Bruce was very, very good. He died of AIDS in 1996 before ever becoming a Pip.

My reliable backup was gone. I stumbled numbly around New York for a couple of years trying to figure out how the people I passed on the street could wear such happy expressions on their faces. Clearly the world had come to an end; why didn't they realize it?

I wished I could just fade away and be done with it.

But director Rob Marshall, gay porn impresario Chi Chi Larue and fate had other plans for me; I became a chorus boy, adult film star "Gus Mattox" and a writer (in that order.)

But what about Bruce? Apart from picking his bones clean for story ideas, how did my late husband fit into my new life A.B. (After Bruce)?

Starting with "Winds From the South" Bruce became a familiar presence on gusmattox.com. I'd slip references to him into my blog and he appeared in the background in several essays. Bruce died fifteen years ago but he continues to inform how I view my own experiences and the world at large. Like the spider swallowed by the Old Lady, he has wriggled and jiggled and tickled his way inside me, becoming an essential part of my being.

Bruce Birnbaum's contribution to the essays and stories in this collection is not insignificant; his spirit provided the backup that enabled me to write them.

I guess you could say Bruce became a Pip after all.

They're Playing Our Song

I seem to be dating again. Not entirely by design, but I've been asked out recently by several attractive guys and I thought it might be interesting to see what I've been missing these past three years. Yes, it's been that long between my last date and this recent flurry. Since being widowed a decade ago I've warbled duets with a feller or three, but we always seem to be singing in different keys. Believe me, I sure can pick 'em.

There was the beautiful blond man who broke up with me because I had never heard of Prada. (I can't really say that I blame him.) After that came the Midwestern transplant with the great chest and the penchant for talking like an eight-year-old, followed by several short affairs that, while brief in duration, were richly saturated with drama. Shall we even mention the man who dumped me when I was out of town with a show and who refused to give back my dog? No, let's not.

The recent medley of Mystery Dates has been uneven, but even though their exterior attributes have been promising (I said "yes" mostly due to their naked pictures online) so far no Prince Charming has opened the door to the accompaniment of 1,000 violins playing the Love Theme from our Major Motion Picture. I'd like to think lightning can strike twice, though; I believe there's a man out there to complete my musical chord. But where is my Major Third? Who is my Dominant 9? Who, indeed?

If someone creates a musical dating service website I will be the first to subscribe. How would it work? I envision posting the usual personal ad info/fiction, but—here's the gimmick—with the addition of the entire playlist from one's iPod. Musical tastes would be analyzed for complementary and discordant overlaps. Knowing in advance what your date listens to could quash any fears that Celine Dion might join you in the bedroom just as things start to get hot and heavy. You don't want Celine's heart going on just as your date is going down.

All this is important because music can do more to the savage beast than just soothe him. Years ago I was having phone sex with some guy from the Upper East Side when, after a pause, he said, "Are you listening to 'Follies?'" I could hear his hardon wilt clear across town.

If I'm really getting back into the dating game I want to know that any potential husbands don't have an iPod crammed full of dance music and Madonna. I'm not judging those selections—the man who listens to all that wouldn't be the one for me, though, and we might as well find it out right off the bat. (I do listen to dance music once in a while but usually when I'm full of substances and/or performing acts the likes of which my mother would heartily disapprove.)

Granted, there are potential pitfalls to my system; based on my iPod playlist my perfect match would be a 53-year-old mother of four from a suburb of Indianapolis. Taking a quick scroll through my tunes I see four versions of "Moon River", tons of Beatles, a smattering of Django Reinhardt and lots and lots of movie soundtracks. If you're the kind of guy who gets a catch in his throat when listening to the bass flute featured in the Love Theme from "Quest for Fire" you can move right in. I'll even clear out a couple of drawers for you. Are my tastes middle of the road? Smack down the double yellow lines, baby. But read between those lines and you'll find some interesting things: oddball Joni Mitchell outtakes, Bryan Ferry doing 1930's standards and Cuban dance bands from between the wars. And it goes without saying, several cuts from the Robert Mitchum calypso album.

It seems like my knowledge of pop music hasn't progressed much since getting that big box of records in the mail ("10 albums for one penny!") from The Columbia Record Club about 30 years ago. If that's the case, so be it. Just don't say you weren't warned if Shelley Duvall singing "He Needs Me" from the "Popeye" soundtrack is playing when you come over for dinner.

I once went on a sex date with a guy because I liked his naked pictures online (see above) but as I climbed the stairs to his apartment I heard coming through the door vintage recordings of cowboy yodeling songs. Wow, I thought; this could be the guy for me! Oddly, I'm drawing a blank right now as to who that was. Hold on. . . hold on. . . Oh, right. That was the guy who ended up stealing my dog.

Maybe iPod Dating® isn't such a hot idea. Maybe I should just stick with the naked pictures.

TRADE WINDS

Wednesday is a big day on the tiny Caribbean island of Saba. Like a movie set in the Old West where the settlers wait around for Wells Fargo, it's the day when the supply boat from St. Maarten comes in. Wednesday morning is a combination delivery pickup and social event. El Momo Cottages, where I was spending the summer, had arriving guests who were expected around 11 AM today so my host Patrick and I headed down to the port about 9:30. On the way down we had a couple of stops to make in "The Bottom," one of the two main settled areas on Saba (Windwardside, where El Momo is located, is the other. Patrick and Sophie call Windwardside "the city," but I think they may have made that up.)

"The Road," however, really is the official name of the one thoroughfare on Saba. It goes from the airport on one side of the island to the port on the other and lies across the mountain like a tangled piece of twine. The switchbacks and turnarounds are legendary because the terrain is so mountainous that it's impossible to go for more than a few meters in a straight line. The inclines and declines also make it pretty tough for one's car to go any further than that without downshifting. On my first trip to The Bottom I found myself clutching the door handle with white knuckles. It's not uncommon to round a steep switchback just to find a car headed in the opposite direction but in the same lane. Most of the cars and trucks here are miniature to compensate for the narrow width of The Road.

We made a stop at the hardware store to try to find light bulbs for some lamps Pat and Sop had brought from Holland. The hardware store is tiny by American standards but is the only game in town on Saba. I noticed a lot of the items on the shelves are the Walmart store brand, Home Goods. But while Sabans may be "living better," they are definitely not "paying less." A tube of silicone caulk? Ten dollars. An eight foot pressure-treated 2x4? Well, that'll set you back a cool twelve bucks. In the grocery store *eight dollars and fifteen cents* buys you a tin of Spam. Since literally everything on the island has to be brought in, the markups are breathtaking.

It turned out Patrick's lamps were fitted with a particular European-size socket. The only option? Travel to St. Maarten—to the French side—and find them there. So the lamps will remain dark until enough things are needed to warrant a trip over. (Again, like the old west.)

After the hardware store we had to stop for gas. The gas station is just outside the port down the hill from The Bottom. The Bottom is something of a misnomer as the road from there to the port drops precipitously. Steep, curvy and constantly threatened with huge boulders that career down the mountain every now and then.

This week Saba is experiencing one of its periodic gas shortages, the reason for which I couldn't quite glean, but it meant that one had to wait in line at *the* gas station and each car was allowed about seven dollars worth of fuel. Until next week. The needle barely moved on the gas gauge, so driving will be kept to a minimum for a while.

The port was hopping; the cargo ship was still in its berth, almost completely unloaded. Cars and small trucks were parked here and there along the quay while their owners caught up with the news since last Wednesday. I witnessed a lot of back-slapping and good-natured ribbing along with some late-morning beer guzzling between unloaded pallets of goods. The men then took their turns retrieving their orders. The atmosphere here—with its combination of salt water and diesel fumes and workers calling to one another from the pier to the ship—brought to mind less an old western and more one of those steamy melodramas from M-G-M about characters getting into each other's way and each other's beds in romantic, remote outposts. "Red Dust," specifically. Griffin, the man in charge, could have been Clark Gable had he been wearing a pith helmet and jodhpurs.

Wielding a clipboard and an authoritative air, he checked the bill of lading and told Patrick the butter he had ordered was in the cooled container on the right-hand side of the ship. Sure, we could just go ahead and get it ourselves. (Imagine that in liability-crazed America!) We climbed onto the ship's deck, dodged a couple of forklifts and walked over to the open door of the mammoth metal box. There at the end of the empty container sat one lonely little parcel: a taped-up cardboard box which originally held packages of Oreos with a hand-written sign taped to it: "El Momo Cottages." In a movie, the image would have been accompanied by a clanging metal echo. We retrieved the butter and hopped back onto the pier.

The other delivery we went to get—a new toaster—was buried somewhere on a pallet but we were on the clock and had to get back to make sure Patrick was there to greet the 11 AM arrivals. So Griffin offered to bring it up to Windwardside with him when his work was done. (As it happens, I just saw him drive by the café where I'm writing this so I may stop by and see if I can get it myself.)

We headed back up The Road, dodging parked cars, oncoming traffic and even wild goats, and made it back to El Momo ahead of the new guests. I always loved those "remote outpost," "tramp steamer," "isolated rubber plantation" black-and-white potboilers I used to watch on the Million Dollar Movie when I was a kid (all of which seem to have featured Thomas Mitchell.) Even then I suspected the situations and locales were overly romanticized and the characters too broadly drawn.

After just one week on Saba I'm not so sure.

HOUSES OF WORSHIP

There is a house in Pennsylvania. Discreetly placed in the forested hills at the western edge of the state, this house was conceived to be one with its environment while simultaneously enhancing its surroundings. It was built as a rarefied place where its owner could spend a few days unencumbered by the pressures of his life as a successful businessman. A house of serenity, this house.

There is another house in Missouri. Standing on the sere, open plains at the western edge of the state this house was not intended to blend into its setting. It was meant to be seen from afar as a beacon for those coming to pay homage to the building itself, and to the cultural phenomenon that financed it. A house of worship, this house.

As might be expected, both houses were conceived and built by men of determination and conviction. Their work was not something they chose to do; they were compelled by forces greater than they. One man by the gods of art and nature, the other by God himself.

Even the names of these buildings summon up ethereal, yet vivid, pictures when spoken aloud.

"*Fallingwater*". Images of a never-ceasing cascade of bountiful water come rushing into one's head; changing with the seasons, yet immutable in its purpose. Much as the water rushes over the exposed Pennsylvania schist, giving the house its name.

The other house is more... well, it's kind of... Alas, my craft fails me when I try to describe this other place. So, I'll let its name speak for itself: "*The Precious Moments Chapel*".

A visit to both houses on the same cross-country drive prompted this writer to ponder how different these buildings—and the emotions they inspire—are, considering the seriousness with which both their creators viewed their commissions.

One afternoon in 1936 in Spring Green, Wisconsin, Frank Lloyd Wright's assistant ran breathless into the master's studio. Edgar Kaufmann, tired of the delays and evasions he had been getting from Wright regarding the plans for his new country house, was on his way from Madison, just over an hour away. Unruffled, Wright tore off the top page from his sketch pad and ran his palms—smooth with age—over the equally smooth vellum. Reaching for a brown pencil he began to sketch planes and shapes. A student poked his head in the door and was "ssshh-ed" by the assistant. Within minutes word spread that something of importance was taking place in the room just off the main dining area, and the drafting table was soon surrounded by eager young men. As Wright formed the last letters of "A House for Edgar Kaufmann" on the drawing, the wheels of a hired Cadillac limousine crunched on the gravel driveway outside. "Please show E.J. into the studio," Wright calmly uttered as he placed the pencil back in its holder.

Midway through Ronald Reagan's second term as president Sam Butcher, a multi-millionaire (thanks to his wide-eyed beige Precious Moments figurines), stood in the center of a crowd of fellow Midwesterners, his neck craned upward to take in the glory of the Sistine Chapel. He whispered to his wife, "Honey, have we got any Tylenol back in the room? I'm gonna have a heck of a headache by the time we get out of here." Then he thought to himself, "Hmmm. . . . a painting on the ceiling. I'll bet I could take that idea and really do something with it." His mind started to race and a dream was born.

A small, nondescript sign on a quiet country road directs one to Fallingwater. The modest parking lot, large enough to hold only the vehicles of the small groups allowed to tour the house at any one time, leads to a tasteful visitor's center. In addition to vintage photographs recounting the history of the house, there is a gift shop that sells monographs of the world's greatest architects. Neutra, Gehry and Mies van der Rohe share shelf space with numerous books on Wright himself. A small concession stand offers cappuccino and biscotti.

The illuminated billboard on the interstate alerts the faithful that they are nearing their destination. Turning onto the secondary road one joins a caravan of cars whose license tags represent a panoply of these United States. Like the Magi drawn by the star, these weary travelers are united in the desire to witness the epitome of what they hold dearest. As uniformed attendants direct private cars to one parking area and chartered buses to another, the Visitor's Center comes into view. A small village, really, the center is accessed by passing a fountain graced by three angels. Three Precious Moments angels. Oh, if they only sold something like this for the yard! Once inside, the streets are lined with quaint shoppes, each selling the same line of merchandise. Let's get a bite before we go into the chapel. I feel faint just thinking about it, and it's been 2 hours since we stopped at the Shoney's breakfast buffet. Just a couple of hot dogs will be fine. Oh, and a diet Pepsi.

Walking down the wooded path, the house comes into view through the trees. The lines of the structure mimic those of the forest, so imposing as it is, one must stand directly in front of the house before the full grandeur of Wright's masterpiece is evident. Entering the almost-hidden front door you find yourself in a small entryway from which you are propelled into a generously proportioned living room. The walls on three sides are made of glass, allowing the woods beyond to become part of the décor. The only sound is the endless splashing of water as it tumbles over the waterfall underneath the house. Wright built the house over the falls, rather than facing them.

Leaving the Visitor's Center, the Chapel stands imposingly in the near distance, at the end of a forecourt lined with Precious Moments topiary figures. The carved wooden doors, featuring (oh, well... you know) open into the vestibule, where organ music is piped in. The guides corral the groups through the sides of the chapel. Traversing the interior perimeter of the chapel one can view Precious Moments-inspired tributes to all the dead (Christian) children who have been "taken too soon", until, through a set of imposing doors, one is thrust into the main chapel. The Mecca of all Pretiosus Momentus.

Little artwork graces the walls at Fallingwater. For one thing, most of the exterior walls are glass, for another, few works of art could compete with the house itself. And, not insignificantly, Wright wanted it that way.

Every inch of wall space is enhanced with murals designed personally by Sam Butcher. The centerpiece of the room is a mural entitled "Hallelujah Square", which depicts multitudes of angel children being welcomed into Heaven and invited to worship at the feet of Jesus Christ, who floats above the scene. The rainbow of facial hues runs the gamut from pale to less pale. But, wait! Yes, there is a little n-, uh, African-American child up there in the corner. Look, that's him—the one playing basketball by himself.

The respectful comments elicited by the visit to Fallingwater are what one might expect from a group touring such a masterpiece: "How much did this place cost?" "I hope it doesn't fall over the edge; at least until we're outa here." "Well, it might be okay if it had comfortable furniture."

Visitors to the chapel, when they can speak at all, offer the kind of sardonic comment one might expect from a group touring such a monument to kitsch: "It's so beautiful. I wish Emma could see this.

You know she has one of the largest collections in the country." "The colors are so bright." "See, George, I told you you'd like art." "I. . . I. . . I'm sorry, I promised myself I wouldn't cry and here I am like a faucet."

Huh?!

To paraphrase P. T. Barnum, no one ever went broke underestimating the taste of the American public. Both Fallingwater and The Precious Moments Chapel, are, in their unique ways, masterpieces. Both are products of men with driven minds and ideas set in cement. Oddly, the buildings share the same exterior color. But, beyond that, the two could not be more dissimilar. At both places I was momentarily filled with rage: in Pennsylvania while listening to the insipid comments and, in Missouri, witnessing the almost sensual outpourings of devotion lavished on such an affront to good taste.

But I do not despair. One can only hope that some future visitor to Fallingwater, dragged there by his/her spouse will look around and think, "Wow, this is pretty cool." And I envision a fine golden day when one of the pilgrim ladies at the Chapel begins to giggle uncontrollably until, gasping for breath, she turns to her friend and says, "When we get back to Minneapolis, Emma, you and I are finally going to that art museum in the park. No, the *modern* one! With the big spoon. Lord, could I use a frank. C'mon!"

AN EMPTY BOWL

There is a water bowl that has been sitting on the front porch of my cabin in the Catskill Mountains for the past year. It's beige earthenware and has D-O-G crudely stenciled on its side. I bought it last year at a Mom and Pop store in Hell's Kitchen after returning from the National Tour of the show "42nd Street." No dog drinks from this bowl, even though it was meant for one: Dan, a cute little terrier mutt I adopted from an actress friend of mine.

Dan had a pretty sketchy history by the time he came to live with me. He appears to be a mix of (mostly) Chihuahua and Border terrier. Picture Toto if he had fallen in with the Bowery Boys and you've got Dan. As a puppy, he was discovered in a prison yard in Hartford, Connecticut by a work-release prisoner named Dan. Dan (the prisoner, not the dog) knew of a woman in town who rescued abandoned animals and then placed them with new owners.

This woman put an ad in the local paper to find Dan (the dog, not the prisoner) a home. The accompanying picture showed a dog with a face and body language that said, "Adopt me... don't adopt me... makes no difference," while his eyes pleaded, "Please, please, *please* take me home!"

My friend Cass succumbed and kept him for 6 of his 7 years. When she gave him to me—because she was traveling too much—she reminded me that Dan "has issues". Don't wear boots around him or he'll turn into the Tasmanian Devil. Don't try to pick him up the wrong way or he'll turn into the Tasmanian Devil. Don't try to scratch his back or... Well, you get the idea.

But, bring out his rope toy and he's as playful as a pup. Scratch his tummy when he runs into the room and rolls over on his back and he's sweet as taffy. And, first thing in the morning, whisper in his ear that it's time to get up and he'll let out a sigh and stretch just as far as he can, sometimes letting out a little squeak as he reaches across the bed to touch your nose with his paw.

Dan and I lived like country squires in my cabin in the woods. He'd lie contentedly in the sun on the front porch, or show his utter disdain for squirrels with a condescending bark. I was going to miss this little fellow being away for a year with the show. But, I knew he'd be okay. I was leaving him in the city with my boyfriend. What could possibly go wrong?

Three months into the tour my boyfriend broke up with me. Let's say I carried 50 percent of the blame and leave it at that.

For the remainder of my time on the road I maintained a mostly one-sided correspondence with the boys back home. Dan and The Ex received Christmas presents and Easter goodies at the fifth-floor walkup on 10th Avenue. I sent money to pay for a year's worth of dog food and always reiterated my intention to have Dan back with me at the cabin when the tour was finished.

Toward the end of the year I got an e-mail from Cass that said, "I don't want to sound paranoid, but ___ wrote me asking about the idea of implanting an I.D. chip under Dan's skin." She talked him out of it, but I had to assume my address was not intended to be on that chip.

It was starting to feel like a Hitchcock thriller starring My Dog.

I refused to believe it. It wasn't a thriller; it was a romantic comedy. Boy meets dog, boy loses dog. . . Returning home from the tour at the end of summer would be the part where boy gets dog back again. Dan and I would walk up the hill to the cabin, stealing affectionate glances at one another, as the sun set and the credits rolled.

But things didn't play out like they do in the movies. I attempted, without success, to get in touch with ___ through e-mail and phone messages. After several weeks of no response I began losing sleep; at the end of a month I was having recurring nightmares. As the leaves on the oaks and maples around the cabin announced the onset of autumn, I found myself at my wits end.

My friend Debby, always a source of solid practical advice, said without hesitation: "____ must be in a bad place to be doing this. You have to think about him and do what's best for him, and, in doing so it will also be what's best for you. You have to give Dan to ____." My heart sank. Then I remembered a proverb I once heard: "The things you keep for yourself are lost for good; the things you give away are *yours forever*."

The course of action seemed clear. I wrote ____:

"After much soul-searching I have decided I need to do what is best for you. And if that means making a gift to you of Dan then that is what I will do. I hope you will allow me to come and say goodbye to him."

I never heard from ____, and I never saw Dan again.

I tried to feel good and angry about it all, but couldn't seem to. Frustrated? Sure. Helpless? You bet. But, one has to be in a deep, dark place to keep someone from saying farewell to his own dog. I might as well have gotten mad at my ex-boyfriend because his eyes are brown and not blue.

The other day I took a load of rubbish to the town dump. Along with a broken lamp and leaky garden hose—other things I don't need anymore—

I left a water bowl with D-O-G stenciled on the side.

The bowl may be gone, but as the proverb says, Dan is mine forever.

HOWARD, WE HARDLY KNEW YE

I read that the Times Square Howard Johnson's is closing its doors after almost fifty years. When I was 18 and moved to West Forty-Fifth Street in 1979, this last Howard Johnson's was going strong. The food was mediocre at best, and none of the twenty-eight flavors of ice cream could match the richness of Haägen-Dazs.

Back then, 9th Avenue was something of a wasteland and HoJo's was the only place to get a late-night snack or a cup of coffee and make "a couple of deals before dawn." At that time of night, the restaurant was usually empty and I had my pick of seats, which was always the same booth in the window that looked out onto 46th Street and the Helen Hayes Theater. The orange vinyl seat would let out a sigh as I settled in.

Moving at a glacial, graveyard-shift pace, the waiter approached, and ignoring my greeting, he'd wipe the table with a wet rag and then place a glass of ice water on the table—overfilled and dripping—along with a laminated menu.

I marvelled at the insouciant style this late-middle-aged African-American man gave to the place. He was a dressed in the regulation uniform of white shirt and black pants, but on any given night, he would be sporting hair from a large collection of toupees. There was the crazy Little Richard style and the Nat "King" Cole (neatly parted and slicked down on the top and sides). My favorite hairpiece, however, was The Nipsey. The Nipsey was a modest yet shapely Afro rising just slightly from the forehead. The waiter didn't seem to choose a toupee to complement his personality, as he didn't appear to have a personality, but I still liked The Nipsey best.

After ordering a dish of peppermint-stick ice cream, I took out a pen and started on the puzzle in the early edition of the Times. I rarely got very far before my imagination would begin to conjure up images of my own name gracing the marquees in the neighborhood. My plan was to be a Broadway composer by age 30. Across the street, at the Helen Hayes, there was a musical version of "Flowers for Algernon" (complete with mouse). So how hard could it be? With my chin in the palm of my hand, I sat gazing out the window into my future when the reflection of my waiter darkened the glass. He placed the metal sundae cup in front of me, filled with already melting ice cream. How did it melt between here and the counter? I didn't care; it contained chips of real peppermint stick and had a fan-shaped wafer cookie stuck into the conical—not spherical—scoop.

I tasted a spoonful, took one last look at the retreating Nipsey, and returned to my 2 A.M. daydream.

I did make it to Broadway, but as an actor, not a composer. That dream is long gone, along with the old Helen Hayes Theater. So, too, is the Broadway that could support a musical version of "Flowers for Algernon." For that matter, so am I, having left Hell's Kitchen over a decade ago. And soon Howard Johnson's will be just a memory as well.

That's New York, I guess.

THE BEAUTY CURSE

My friend Tim and I were browsing the profiles on BigMuscle.com the other day, consigning the especially attractive men to horrible fates: a fatal disease here, a terrible disfiguring accident there. You know what I mean—the kinds of things that guys imagine when confronted with particularly demoralizing beauty. This God-play knew no geographical restrictions; there seem to be stunning specimens of maleness in every region of the U.S. Heck, we even found a few fer'ners destined for the rack (once Tim and I take over the world, that is.)

I'd pull up a profile picture and wait for Tim's reaction. "Oh, my god, he's gorgeous. I hate him." Tim would point out an attractive face or bicep and I'd respond with, "Amazing. Beautiful. His days are numbered." Then we closed the Powerbook, sunk back on the couch and sighed in tandem as Tim opened another bag of chips and I reached for the remote to flip back and forth between Paula's Home Cookin' and the "Diff'rent Strokes" E! True Hollywood Story.

As another stick of butter melted away in Paula's skillet Tim shook an accusing finger in the direction of the computer which lay on the coffee table and asked, "Those, uh, those *guys* on that website. . . Do you think their lives are just perfect? Do you think they've just got everything they need and are happier than shit?" My knee-jerk response was to say, "No, they're just a bunch of fucking assholes and are probably miserable," but after what that poor Gary Coleman went through I was feeling a little more charitable than usual.

I pondered Tim's question as I licked the orange cheese dust from my fingers.

Yeah, I suppose the really gorgeous, Adonis-like guys have a leg up on some things in life. They may get served first at a crowded bar. They're invited to hang out with others of their ilk on the beach. The shirt that looks great on the mannequin will look just as good on them when they get it home from the store.

But are their lives better simply because they've been graced with good looks? I don't think so. We assume the Chelsea Boys and the WeHo guys lead lives far more interesting and exciting than our own because we *want* to think they do. Believing the pretty boys not only have fabulous faces and bodies, they also have fabulous lives in which to display them gives us yet another reason to resent them, to beat ourselves up about it. We almost *need* them to live wonderful lives to help explain the normalness of our own. We'd be just as special if we were that beautiful, too. Right?

But the majority of the beauties we see everywhere lead average lives. Why? Simply because most people are average. (That is, after all, why it's called "average.") They have attainable ambitions which they muse on in Ikea apartments. They have uninspired opinions on forgettable movies and possess a small shelf of books, all of which, besides "The DaVinci Code", are emblazoned with a large "O" on their covers.

There's nothing wrong with a life like this. It's a life—with subtle variations—not unlike that of most Americans. When it's lived by a Beautiful Man, however, a man who we expect to be a superior being—as superior as his physical appearance—it seems banal and meaningless. "That isn't how someone who looks like a movie star lives! That's how *I* live!"

We go directly from hating these guys because they're better than us simply because of their looks to hating them because they're *no* better than us even *with* their looks. We wouldn't feel contemptuous of a bland looking guy who leads a bland life because we probably wouldn't think twice about him in the first place. A bland person can be bland anonymously while a beautiful man is bland in a spotlight. It's that variable of "beauty" that makes them susceptible to increased scrutiny.

I've seen a similar phenomenon at work in the porn industry. My own anecdotal research suggests that the principal assumptions about guys in porn is that they're dumb. I would have to concur; most of the men working in the adult film industry are not brilliant. Most of the kids in the chorus of "42nd Street", in which I appeared (no, as a *principal*, darling) also were not brilliant. When I worked at Pizza Hut in high school none of my coworkers were sending rockets to the moon. Because (altogether now) most people are average.

But the guys in porn possess an even more volatile variable than the beautiful guys: *we masturbate to them.* For the ten or fifteen minutes (OK, the hour or so) we watch a porn flick we are so invested in the men in the scene that they actually serve as our sexual proxy. How could we lower ourselves to blow a load over someone who's nothing but a big dope? In our minds we make these guys stupider than they really are to explain away our lust.

Are there good-looking, in-shape men who are intelligent and thoughtful, in happy, fulfilling relationships with jobs that further the welfare of mankind? Sure there are. And are there porn stars who are dumb as posts with nothing much to brag about other than a big dick and a flexible pelvis? Believe you me—they're out there.

Tim clicked his tongue against the roof of his mouth and sighed. "But we shouldn't assume anything about either of those groups because prejudging anyone about anything is unfair to them and counterproductive to our own self-esteem," he sing-songed with the half-hearted enthusiasm of a teenager promising to have the car home by midnight.

"I guess so," I shrugged.

"Oh great! Just as I was working up a really nasty punishment for ItalynMsclStud.

Sorry, Tim. Let's assume from now on that the beautiful guys and the porn guys are just average fellows like us trying to get through the day in one piece. The beauty they're cursed with really doesn't make it any easier for them in the long run.

Those trust fund babies, on the other hand ...

THE CHURCH OF ME

A lot of the guys I worked with in porn were ostensibly heterosexual. It's something that has long puzzled me and, after reading a fascinating interview in the Dallas Voice with former porn star (and personal favorite, I hasten to add) Tom Katt, I'm even more confused. Katt, who now goes by David Papaleo (surely a name ripe for changing—who could remember that at the video rental counter?) is not only through with porn, he's gone straight and—here's the kicker—found Jesus. He's even considering joining the clergy.

To give Mr. Popodopolous his due, he doesn't seem to have a problem with homosexuals or bisexuals or the kind of sex those groups engage in, it's just not for him. "'If you are naturally heterosexual and you're having sex with men, well, first, you're treating that guy unfairly,' he says." My friend Bradley, who enjoys being treated unfairly by straight men, would dispute that point, but I know what he's getting at. As for Mr. Popinfresh's current orientation, "I identify as heterosexual. There was a time I thought of myself as bisexual, and I never hide that fact."

I suppose the process of coming to terms with one's sexual orientation varies with the individual and sometimes can stretch over years. I personally had a "Eureka!" moment when I discovered I was able to fold a fitted sheet into a perfect square. That can't be learned.

He goes on to say that gay marriage is "not wrong" and that he's not ashamed of his work in videos. Pretty progressive thinking for a born-again type, all in all. While I myself am a staunch atheist and believe that organized religion is the root cause of most of the horrors the world has known, I fully support Mr. Penelopepitstop's quest for personal fulfillment and understanding. I might differ with his (newly) negative views on gay porn but I'm going to cut him a little extra slack. And the fact that his nipples drive me insane has nothing to do with it and I resent the implication.

But this does raise a broader question: why does a "redeemed" soul, after a life of sex/drugs/crime or crime/drugs/sex or crime/crime/ drugs/politics or drugs/politics/sex/drugs/crime, always wind up at the feet of Jesus Christ? Why do J.C. and his Dad always get to be the Last Exit Before Toll on the Highway to Eternal Damnation? Born-agains praise the Lord for giving them a new chance at life; He is always given credit for the good things in the world while mankind seems content to take the blame for the bad. There's an old show business saying, "If you believe the good reviews you also have to believe the bad reviews." While you're on your knees thanking God for clearing up that annoying rash remind him he kind of fucked up big-time with Hurricane Katrina.

No, I'd think twice before handing myself over to the aleatory whims of the Big Christian God.

Which begs the question, how come nobody— Sammy Davis, Jr. aside—converts to Judaism as the cleanser for a dissipated life? And why is religion—any religion—the default concept to "find" when pursuing redemption? Why not "find" something like—oh, I don't know—something like... *fudge*. A pound-and-a-half of chocolate fudge with walnuts would set me on the straight and narrow for sure. Or how about praying to a Technics Dual Cassette Deck with Auto-Reverse? A gadget like that, with its ability to play forever without stopping, offers the acolyte a clear and true vision of infinity. But if it must be a personage, why not somebody like, say, Rickie Lee Jones? Now, *there's* a deity that would keep you on your toes. You could never be sure if she would offer you blessed salvation or try to steal twenty bucks from your wallet. You'd be so busy watching your back you wouldn't have time to indulge in any vices.

I'm just not buying this Born Again business as an antidote to profligacy and corruption. I believe there are some things that are simply innate that even the Gospels can't dispel. Years ago a good friend of mine who was an ex-everything addict (and a really big queen) started behaving mysteriously and eventually came out of the closet as a Mormon/heterosexual convert. As we left the restaurant after our farewell lunch before shedding his old life completely I asked about the crazy lady who lived next door. "I feel like I'm Olivia DeHavilland in 'The Snake Pit,'" he complained. "Girl," I said, draping a friendly arm on his shoulder, "there's not a straight man in the history of the world who has ever referenced 'The Snake Pit.'"

Like Mr. Papardelle, I have recently left the world of gay porn to pursue other interests. Unlike him I still hold the industry and the people in high regard. I'm not joining the clergy; I'm going back to the theater. But it's funny, just like David Papaleo (the former Tom Katt,) Tom Judson (the former Gus Mattox) will be appearing before the multitudes, donning representative garb and declaiming from a sacred text.

Can my own church be far behind?

THE LONGEST MILE

The parking lot behind the theater in Provincetown is never quiet; the exhaust fan from the café runs 24/7 and there's always either a vehicle or a bicycle entering or leaving.

But the image that has really tickled me over the summer is brought on by the surface of the lot itself; a medium-size gravel. It's not my beloved Item 4, which eventually compacts into a solid mass. It's a loose, gray stone roughly the size of Kraft Caramels. It shifts here and there based on the 3-, 4-, 5- and 6-point turns that vehicles must make to facilitate driving forward through the narrow alley rather than having to back precariously into the very busy street.

Sometimes, if I'm not really paying attention, I'm fooled into thinking there's a light rain falling outside when the gravel is trod upon.

But beginning in the late-afternoon—every day—when I can often be found reading on my porch, I get to witness a lovely and unique procession: The Art House Drag Queens. Many of the acts booked here at The Art House are, in fact, drag acts. For that matter, a good percentage of the shows all over town feature male performers in fabulous female garb. Clearly, it's one of the things visitors expect when they come to this last town on the Cape.

Since all of us performers have to promote our shows by handing out fliers on the street ("barking" is what we call it) the drag acts have to spend countless extra hours in makeup and costume. God bless 'em, I say.

So 'round about 5 o'clock, depending on the lineup that evening, the Ladies start to trickle out from the dressing rooms, which are behind my apartment near the stage door. And this is the part of which I'm so enamored: most of these gals sport precariously high heels for optimum dramatic effect. But high heels + gravel doth not a happy marriage make! So I drop my book to my lap and peer over my (2.00 strength) dollar store reading glasses and watch unseen as the queens traipse across the expanse of gravel to the brick paved sidewalk at the street end of the alley. It's about 50 feet from the dressing room area to the bricks and depending on the heels (and the confidence of the Ladies) the voyage can be tricky or, well, trickier. I hear them as they march confidently up the concrete ramp from behind the theater and step onto the loose stones.

And at that point the pace slows to a crawl. They focus their gaze on the ground ahead. Weight is shifted from the heels to the balls of their feet.

Ankles wobble. Hands are deployed to the side—highwire-like—to achieve balance. Some delicately arc one foot in front of the other like great plumed birds. Others glide their feet mere centimeters above the ground. But no matter their individual techniques, they are all Elizas on the ice crossing the river of gravel to the distant brick-paved shore.

And here is the glorious part: the instant those size 12 slippers hit solid ground, these wary creatures (that up to this moment very distinctly resembled nothing but men wearing dresses) swan out into the street as poised, regal, confident, fabulous *Drag Queens*.

And all's right with the world.

A MILLION MEN

A million is a vague concept to most people; one seldom encounters a tangible example of just what those seven digits represent. Dennis Bell, who recently acquired the complete assets of the Athletic Model Guild, understands all too well the scope of that number; he's got about a million men in his storeroom, waiting to be counted.

AMG was (and is) the parent company of "Physique Pictorial," the publication instantly recognizable for its sublimely artificial tableaux of young men in posing straps engaging in not-so-innocent horseplay. Cowboys and Roman Centurions made regular appearances in its pages, setting the stage—and standard—for gay sex fantasies for decades to come. Primarily a one-man operation (Bob Mizer, its founder, shot every one of the images and each of the thousands of 16mm films and videotapes), the catalog spans nearly sixty years and introduced many a young man to the beauty of the male body.

One of those young men was Wisconsin-born-and-bred Bell, who encountered a discarded stash of Physique Pictorials one afternoon in a ditch on his walk home from school. He, in turn, hid them away himself (presumably the preferred method of most collectors over the years) little imagining what a central role those pictures would come to play in his adult life.

Little Dennis grew up and became a photographer in his own right, making a living shooting, well, naked men. Working for such adult studios as Hot House, Titan and Falcon (which is where I first encountered him) he became adept at adjusting his own style to the needs of the different companies. This, in turn, paid off when producing his own work. Dennis was not only a devotee of Bob Mizer's beefcake shots, he found he was able to mimic the look and style of those classic images on his own, continuing the tradition without actually trying to recreate what had already been done to perfection.

The success of Bell's first physique-related website convinced him that interest in physique photos and the Athletic Model Guild had not dimmed in the years since Mizer's death.

Learning of the availability of the AMG catalog, Bell decided the time was right to introduce this piece of history to a new generation. Surprisingly, the entire catalog—negatives, films, videos, magazines, even some recognizable props—was intact. Bell purchased the lot and found himself with a huge amount of material that needed to be moved somewhere.

The storeroom at the Athletic Model Guild offices resembles a Kodak warehouse: thousands of yellow boxes line scores of shelves containing just under one million negatives. The sheer number took the new owner somewhat by surprise. "As I unpacked the collection, I kept buying more shelving to hold the boxes." Fortunately for history Bob Mizer was meticulously organized. "Today's digital photography storage and cataloging systems are way beyond Bob's system," says Bell. "He used an alpha-numeric system, starting with A-1, A-2, A-3 etc. When he reached the end of Z, he continued at ZA1, ZA2, . . . ZB1, ZB2, and so forth. This gives a final image ID number of something like XV23-AS."

So even though the system doesn't describe the contents of each image, "the negatives are organized enough that if I have a model name or image number, I can go into the archive stack and find that image within a couple minutes. There is also a card catalog that was kept with every model who was shot, and [whatever images] that model made."

Some of those models went on to become known in other avenues. Along with Andy Warhol superstar Joe D'Allesandro and Dennis Cole (future husband of Charlie's Angel Jaclyn Smith), "Arnold (Schwarzenegger) posed for Bob in the AMG compound just about 2 years after the

Pumping Iron movie was made in 1973. . . showing an incredible set of muscles in a leopard print swimsuit."

Ideally, the AMG staff will eventually include a pair of archivists to catalog and digitize the collection. "Only about three thousand have been digitized," in the fourteen months since Bell acquired them, "enough for the new website member section. The entire process could take 3-5 years." After converting every image, the original negatives will be stored under archival conditions, with the digital files used for prints and publishing.

Several of the 10,000+ models who posed for Bob Mizer have gotten in touch with Bell and the AMG—mostly through the internet—some of them decades after the original photo shoots. Dennis is actively pursuing more such contacts and meetings. In addition to providing the models with prints, he hopes to produce a video documentary in which the men recount their experiences posing for Physique Pictorial.

But, under Dennis Bell's watchful eye, the Athletic Model Guild is looking to the future as much as it is preserving its own storied past. His plans for the company and its assets were instrumental in convincing the Mizer estate to sell him the materials. In addition to re-issuing the existing images and films, Dennis is drawing on his own experience in the adult film industry to carry-on and expand the AMG brand. "Although Bob tried to film hardcore in the 1970s, he wasn't extremely successful at it. The difference between me and Bob is our experience working with hardcore. With my experience, AMG will now be able to produce full sexual situations that Bob couldn't do."

While the reincarnated Athletic Model Guild has all the tools of the digital age at its disposal it is, essentially, still the dreamchild of one man. The symmetry of such a collection passing from the hands of photographer and pioneer Bob Mizer into those of photographer and entrepreneur Dennis Bell has its romantic aspects, but, "right now it is all I do, my social life is gone. But I know that soon we'll be back in production, and I'll start shooting again."

Until then Dennis Bell spends his solitary days in the company of a million men.

LITTLE MISS INDIAN GIVER

The first birthday party I recall with any clarity occurred when I was in kindergarten. Perhaps the reason I remember this one is that it would have been my first party where the attendees were children other than my sisters and cousins. The guest list was most likely comprised of my friends from school, in addition to my family.

But, the real reason the party on my 5th birthday has stuck in my mind all these years can be summed up in two words: Theresa Duurloo. She was my best friend in kindergarten. We'd pal around on the playground and share a cot for our nap. If Terry didn't want her second graham cracker, I was the lucky recipient—no one else even bothered to ask. I guess she was my first girlfriend.

So, when my mother asked whom I wanted at my party, Theresa was, naturally, at the top of the list. I invited one or two other little friends from school and my sisters and cousins rounded out the guest list.

We hadn't built the addition on our house at this point, so the extra leaf was put in the kitchen table and the whole thing was dragged into the living room. We all had party hats and noisemakers and the paper plates matched the napkins.

The cake had been made special: Mom had a little booklet put out by Baker's Coconut that had directions to create festive-shaped cakes by cutting round and square cake layers and piecing them together. Patterns were included and all of the cakes had coconut sprinkled on top of the frosting. There were plans for a bunny, a locomotive and a clown, among many others, but I asked Mom to make the sailboat cake for me.

A square cake was cut on an angle in two unequal halves to create the sails. The hull of the boat featured coconut dyed blue, with Life Saver portholes and a licorice whip mast. The sails billowed with a snowy coconut covering and five candles were placed along the bottom edge of the cake.

After cake and ice cream came the opening of the presents. I have forgotten everything I received that day except for one very special present: Theresa Duurloo gave me a blue Tonka Toys Jeep. I loved it! It was my favorite of all my presents.

When the other kids mother's came to pick them up and the party started winding down, I went to find my new Jeep so I could hold it while saying goodbye to my guests. But, it was nowhere to be found! I looked everywhere for my Jeep, but it had vanished. I ran into the hall, panic-stricken, just as Mrs. Duurloo arrived to pick up Terry. Alarmed by the look on my face, my mother asked what was wrong. "I can't find my blue Jeep," I cried.

The mothers looked at each other, then they looked at Theresa, who stood at the door looking like butter wouldn't melt in her mouth.

"Theresa, what's under your coat?" asked Mrs. Duurloo. Terry went on to explain that she had merely brought the Jeep for me to play with and fully intended to bring it back home with her. Her attitude implied that it was clearly a quality item and she surely couldn't be expected to leave it here with a . . . boy.

The mothers started to laugh, the children began to cry and Mrs. Duurloo left the party with her daughter and without the Jeep. I have it to this day, in fact.

Twelve years later, Theresa Duurloo and I found ourselves the only two members of our kindergarten class who were still in the same school district and graduating together. We met in the parking lot of the school after the ceremony. With our robes billowing in the soft June breeze we hugged each other, holding on to our caps as they knocked into each other as we embraced.

She put her mouth next to my ear and whispered, "Y'know, I never did forgive you for keeping that Jeep." And with that, we pulled apart and said our final goodbyes before going off to separate parties and separate lives.

RIGATONI WITH SAUSAGE AND FENNEL

1 pound rigatoni
5 Italian sausages
2 fennel bulbs, stalks removed, feathery
     ends set aside.
chicken stock
olive oil, salt & pepper to taste, handful
     fresh dill (chopped together with the
     feathery ends of the fennel), grated
     parmigiano reggiano
1 bottle good champagne

1. Heat a large, heavy skillet on medium-high heat and place sausages in it. Split the sausages with a knife and, using a wooden spoon, force the meat out of the casings. I use turkey sausage for this recipe because it's ostensibly less awful for you. Also, I get naked in front of a camera from time to time, so any place I can save on my fat intake is good. Besides, I saw this documentary called "American Dream" about the Hormel packing plant strike and, jeez, what goes on in meat processing plants is gross.

2. Contemplate the sad fate of cattle and the like as you pour a glass (preferably a flute) of champagne

and drink to the turkeys that have found their ground-up way into your pan.

3. When the sausage is browned and cooked through, transfer it to a bowl and set aside. Cut the fennel bulbs in half and cut out the core. Slice them from top to bottom (or side to side if you're feeling contrary; you're certainly not going to hurt *my* feelings if you do) and throw them into the hot pan, where you've placed a couple of tablespoons of olive oil. Take a piece of fennel from the pan and marvel at how well it goes with champagne as you take another sip.

4. Once the fennel is caramelized add the sausage and keep cooking. Throw in half the dill and add a cup or so of the stock. When the stock reduces add some more. When the champagne in your glass reduces, add some more to that, too.

5. Let out a yelp as the twice-risen bread dough falls to the floor and the dish shatters. Curse the god-damn bad luck of it all and say, "Oh, well, good thing I didn't put the pasta in yet". See if everyone needs a refill and announce that you're not going to let a minor setback like this ruin your dinner party and that you'll make a fresh batch *stat!* Ignore the protestations of your guests and open a second bottle of champagne.

6. When the dough is ready to go into the oven put the pasta into the boiling water. Add some more chicken stock to the pan and let reduce as the pasta cooks. For that matter, go ahead and throw a ladle of the pasta water into the pan as well. I don't know why, but they do it on TV and it makes it look like you know what you're doing.

7. Drain the cooked pasta and put it back into the pot along with the sauce, the rest of the dill and the grated cheese. Give it a good stir and transfer to a serving bowl. Place on the table and shrug modestly as your guests ooh and ahh. "Oh, I just threw it together", goes nicely with this dish, along with a green salad.

8. Jump up from the table when you realize the bread is burning in the oven and tell your guests they've been eating too many carbs, anyway.

9. Sit back down and finish the meal.

HIM AND HIS SHADOW

The phone rang twice before I could answer it. Could I do an overnight? In Pennsylvania?

I'm not fond of overnight jobs. They're inherently risky, for one thing. If you and the client don't click and decide to call it off, you're forced into an uncomfortable renegotiation for the time you've spent together. If the client doesn't appeal to you, you've got to put on the act for hours longer than normal. But, the real reason I try to avoid overnight gigs is that *I don't like morning sex.* I jump out of bed upon waking. I want my coffee and I want to read the paper. I don't want to kiss anybody before I've brushed my teeth.

But, there's this arts-and-crafts sideboard I've had my eye on and a quick thousand bucks would somewhat alleviate my guilt if I were to buy it.

Oh, okay. Sure, I'll do it.

The client wanted to chat a bit before our date. I hate feeling like I'm giving it away over the phone, but for a thousand dollars you get a little extra. We arranged to meet two days later and he told me about where he lived; he was a college professor in Pennsylvania, just a little older then me, and lived near the university in a house he had just had built. He lived there with his brother.

And did his brother know why I would be coming? "He thinks we met through a personal ad and this is our first date." What does your brother do? He's a professor, too? Computer science, both of you? Interesting.

That Friday was gray and rainy. As I drove from Manhattan into the wilds of Pennsylvania I tried to put a positive light on things. I had never been to this part of the state before, and the guy had to be intelligent, at least, if he was a professor at the university there.

After leaving the Turnpike I drove across the state towards, and then through town. The directions my client had provided soon found me in an area that was strangely barren; the wooded suburbs of the picturesque college town seemed to end abruptly and left me driving through a flat, treeless district. The rain had let up and the late-afternoon sun sent frail rays through the greasy gray clouds, coating the oil-slicked road with a weak film of autumnal light. In the distance I saw four houses—two on either side of the road—lined up perfectly flat with the street on which they sat. The street sign told me this was my destination.

As I drew closer I saw these weren't just houses; these were mansions. Brand new, immaculately finished behemoths that sat close enough to one another to expose the underlying plans for each house as identical. Only the exterior details provided enough distinction to keep the occupants from entering the wrong domicile on a foggy evening. There were spindly young trees with twin upright supports planted here and there in the yards. Seams still showed between the strips of new sod.

I turned into the arcing blacktopped driveway and pulled up to the front door under the twin-columned portico. My two-door vintage convertible suddenly felt Lilliputian in front of this monumental edifice. I turned off the ignition, got out and walked around the front of the car and up the two broad front steps. Within moments of ringing the bell, one half of the wide, double door silently swung open.

There stood my date. He wore brown loafers, khaki pants and a pink button-down collar shirt as well as a very obvious blond toupee. That'll be a challenge I thought, as I planned my strategy of never touching his head. But it was his skin that made the strongest impression. It was translucent as alabaster. I couldn't quite call him an albino, but his white skin and blue eyes, pale as dead hydrangea, gave him an eerie, ethereal quality that reminded me of the evil children in the movie *Village of the Damned*. I tried desperately to remember how that film ended as I reached out my hand and introduced myself.

"Hi, Scott. I'm Gus."

"You found it okay, I see."

I looked at the floor to keep my gaze from drifting upward to his hair and saw a shadow flicker behind the door. Scott must have noticed my glance.

"Oh. This is my brother, Mark."

From behind the other half of the front door stepped a carbon copy of my client. Everything was identical except that he wore a blue Oxford cloth shirt, not the same pink as his brother.

"I . . . guess you guys are twins," I offered with a chuckle to cover my surprise, as I confirmed with a quick look that even the toupees were the same. "Nice to meet you, Mark. Are you joining us for dinner?"

I've always had a fantasy of having sex with twin brothers, but, now that the pieces were falling into place for that possibility, I was having doubts that this was the pair. It was going to be a job keeping interest in just one of these guys; two would tax my abilities beyond endurance.

"No, I'm staying in tonight," answered Mark as he took a handkerchief from his pocket and sneezed into it.

"Well, Scott, should we get going," I asked as Mark hovered in the vestibule.

"I thought I'd show you around the house before we go, if that's okay."

Scott and Mark then proceeded to give me a guided tour of their house. There was a billiard room downstairs complete with a double green glass-shaded lamp hanging above the felt surface of the table and cues lined up perfectly in their holder on the wall.

"Do you guys play?"

They answered "no" in unison.

There was a music room upstairs. The ivory-colored Wurlitzer sat peacefully in a corner, snug on the white carpet. I noticed there were no indentations in the broadloom where the feet of the bench would have rested were a player sitting on it. There was also no piano music to be seen anywhere.

"Do you guys play?"

They looked at one another and then at me.

"No," answered Scott. "No, neither of us play," echoed Mark.

My eye traveled to a marble chess set atop a reproduction Chippendale mahogany game table placed artfully in front of the picture window. Two identical kings stared at each other across the board. The chairs were set at an inviting angle, as if to say, "Come, spend an afternoon contemplating the intrigues of this ancient game."

"Do you guys. . . " I looked in Scott's eyes and, seeing nothing, continued, ". . . want to show me the upstairs?"

Returning from dinner the windshield wipers of the sedan maintained a steady *thup-thup. . . thup-thup.* We pulled into the driveway of the house and around to the side, where I had re-parked my car at Scott's request before leaving for the restaurant.

During dinner the talk had flowed effortlessly. The double martini had inspired me and the conversational ball never dropped. Perhaps I was trying to postpone the inevitable by keeping up an endless banter. The pale blond man across the table looked directly at me for most of the meal, and never seemed to blink. Scott was perfectly pleasant, but I was not looking forward to climbing into bed with him. As the tires of the car hummed along the damp pavement my hand felt for the comforting outline of the diamond-shaped blue pill in my pocket.

The automatic garage door closed behind us. After stepping out of the car onto the immaculate cement floor we met in front of the three-pronged medallion on the hood and stood facing each other. I smiled uncomfortably as Scott leaned toward me and placed a tentative kiss on my closed mouth. As he pulled away I felt the cool snap of wetness where his lips had left a trace of saliva.

The dishwasher was running as we entered the house through the dark kitchen. The flickering blue light of a television and the soft murmur of a laugh track emanated from the "media room" across the hall. Scott took my hand and led me in that direction. His palm felt moist and his grasp timid. We stopped in the doorway and Mark looked up from his program. Holding up an index finger he drew in several quick short breaths and then sneezed into his handkerchief.

"Sorry. How was dinner?"

"Terrific. Your brother's a fun date."

"We'll see you in the morning, Mark," said Scott. He nodded to his brother and once again took my hand and led me to the wide, carpeted stairs.

In the bathroom I swallowed the Viagra before showering. With my head bowed under the hot spray I reminded myself of the sideboard this night would allow me to buy. I wrapped a towel around my waist and opened the door. Scott was waiting just on the other side, still fully dressed, and, averting his gaze, slid by me into the bathroom as I passed him and headed down the hall.

The sheets were cool and fresh and I looked around the room as I waited for Scott to come back from the bathroom. The chintz wallpaper matched the fabric that covered the round table in the corner of the room. Several gilt picture frames sat on the table, and I noticed the pictures they held were the stock images of happy families and couples used to display the frames in the store. Nothing in the room gave any clue to either the sex or age of its occupant. I imagined Scott walking in to a furniture store and saying I'll take the whole room, thanks.

I heard the bathroom door close and footsteps padding softly toward the bedroom. "Are you ready," asked Scott from the other side of the door. "I'm in bed," I answered. A pale, delicate hand reached in the door and turned off the light from the switch on the wall.

The room was now totally dark.

I felt the covers being drawn back and the whisper of a body sliding into bed. Scott reached over and began stroking my stomach, his hand traveling up to my chest. Then I felt breath on my face as Scott brought his mouth to mine and placed a dull kiss on my lips. He slipped his tongue in my mouth and left it there, waiting for me to take control.

Just then I felt the first flush of the Viagra. I'll get through this, I thought.

Scott climbed onto my dick and began to fuck himself. I tried to focus on the physical sensation. Neither of us made a sound; the entire experience was silent.

By the time he returned from the bathroom with a wet towel to wipe the cum from my stomach I had started to fall asleep. He thanked me and turned on his side, facing away from me. Sliding closer I positioned myself behind him and draped my arm over his soft, toneless body. I reached my hand up to tug his ear but overshot my mark and felt a coarse, straw-like substance that I realized was his hair. I quickly lowered my hand and tried not to shudder as sleep finally overtook me.

Sometime later I was awakened by the sound of the bedroom door opening. The darkness of the room told me it was still the middle of the night. A crescent of light crept in from the hall through the open door as Scott's silhouette returned from the bathroom. "Sorry I woke you," he said as he slid into bed.

I mumbled something in response and closed my eyes again. In a moment I felt a hand on my thigh. Oh, no. The only thing worse than morning sex is middle-of-the-night sex. I sighed to myself and realized that for a thousand dollars the guy was entitled to more than just one quick fuck.

There was still enough Viagra in my system to give me a quick erection when Scott began to stroke my penis. I put my hands behind my head and attempted to conjure up something sexy enough to make my hardon last through the blow-job. Scott lay on his side, masturbating as he sucked my dick, and soon I indicated with my breathing that I was close to orgasm. He pulled his mouth away and I shot on my stomach as he reached a climax.

After cleaning up I handed the towel to Scott and turned on my side away from him. He pulled the covers up and settled in for sleep.

And then he sneezed.

My eyes snapped open in the darkness. Was Scott coming down with Mark's cold, or had they switched places in the night?

"Scott?"

"Yes?"

"You okay?"

"Uh-huh."

"Okay. G'night."

I lay there wondering if I had just had sex with the other twin. Not exactly how I had hoped to fulfill that fantasy of mine, but interesting, nonetheless. Of course, there was the issue of whether they were getting something for nothing. I'm not a multiplex, after all; you can't buy one ticket and then sneak into the movie next door. I tried—and failed—to imagine how I might raise the subject, and then let the notion slip out of my head into the black night.

A gentle pressure on my shoulder awakened me as Scott (Mark?) stood over me to say that breakfast was waiting down in the kitchen. He was already showered and fully dressed. I rubbed my eyes and mumbled that I'd be down in a few minutes as I watched him close the bedroom door and leave the room.

The twins were whispering to each other as I entered the kitchen. They were not dressed identically this morning. One of them put his cup down on the granite countertop and walked to the coffee pot.

"Coffee, Gus?"

I nodded yes and watched as his delicate hands lifted the pot from its holder and tipped it to pour the steaming liquid into a fresh cup, which he then handed to me.

"Half and half and sugar on the table. . . "

I sat at the table and selected a muffin from the woven straw basket full of baked goods. The towel lining the basket was of the same blue-striped cotton as the tablecloth. The twins then joined me at the table, one sitting on either side of me. Mark (Scott?) poured orange juice into three glasses before distributing them.

I lifted the glass, the parallel rings etched into the surface creating an alternating smooth/rough sensation in my hand. I looked from one identical face to the other and raised my glass in front of me. After a moment's pause I toasted them; *"Vive la difference,"* I uttered, and swallowed the tangy liquid in one gulp. Mark and Scott looked at me and then at each other and then they drank their orange juice.

The men stood in the entryway as I pulled away from their enormous house. The double door was fully open to allow them to stand side by side and they waved to me before turning back inside. I watched in the rear-view mirror as the two halves of the door swung closed and met to become one complete unit.

My mind mulled over the previous evening's events as I approached the Holland Tunnel in the light Saturday morning traffic. Sailing through the tollbooth as the sensor read my pre-paid tag I looked up and caught a glimpse of the twin towers of the World Trade Center just as my car entered the tile-lined tunnel that would take me to Manhattan and home.

RECOUNTING THE ABBOTTS

With Apologies to Ruth Draper. . .

Hello? . . . Well, good morning. . . Oh, my, it *was* a fantastic night. *I* was a participant in the 2005 George Abbott Awards for Excellence in the Theater presented to Rob Marshall, Kathleen Marshall and Harvey Fierstein! I'm still recovering. Not even out of bed yet, to be honest. You know how these benefits are; fun but exhausting. . . Details, details, it *is* all about details with you, isn't it? Very well, I'll be happy to tell you about the evening. Well you know, we opened the show with that charming "Wilkommen" from "Cabaret" that Robbie choreographed. A slightly shorter version, of course. . . What? Yes I dragged out the old alto sax for the occasion. Thank god there was a reed in the case. I haven't played it since last fall. . . No, my dear, we had *one* rehearsal a few days before. Yes, just the one. . . It's called "professionalism", darling. You wouldn't know about that. . . Joking. . . I'm *joking*! You know I have the ultimate respect for your cruise ship work. . . So demanding, all that rolling as you come out of the Panama Canal and all. . . Yes, I *do* remember hearing all about your rendition of "Memory" while wearing taps. Legendary, really. Anyway, darling, the evening closed with a bunch of us gypsies singing "So Long, Farewell" because, well, I'm sure you know, Robbie and Kathleen Marshall's first job in the theater was playing two of those charming Von Trapp children in Pittsburgh... Yes, *Pittsburgh...* Kathleen? Well, my dear, she never looked lovelier. I've always thought she resembled a younger, more lithe Tammy Grimes. So much like Tammy, don't you think?... Yes, I suppose you would have to add "but sane" to that list. You *are* wicked. We do love *la Grimes*, though, don't we? Simply *worship* her... Now, where was I? Oh, of course, the finale... we had one very quick rehearsal just before the event to stage the number... Come again? Oh, about three dozen of us, I suppose... Yes, it *was* like the Von Trapps had gone Mormon or something! Row upon row of pivot-step-march-march-march... Who was in it? Well, you know those gypsies; lots of faces one recognizes, but one is never sure from where. There did seem to be one large group who all knew each other or were in one show together or something. I don't really know because they kept to themselves... Oh, I *tried*, darling. You know me: a regular Pearl Mesta when it comes to a meet-and-greet... No, they just weren't having me... Oh, now stop! There were *not* more Tony Awards than brain cells among them. No, I won't have you speak ill of dancers... Well, because it's just too easy, that's why... Well, yes, we *were* invited to the event as guests, not just as the entertainment. It was interesting going to a job in my suit and carrying my casual clothes to wear in the number, rather than the other way around... Oh, it's *too true*; one simply wants to take a tray of canapes and make the rounds. Yes, it's in one's blood I suppose. Ah well... Black tie, of course... Mostly just your basic tux. A questionable waistcoat here and there, perhaps... Me? Well, no, I don't own a tux anymore, I'm afraid... That Calvin Klein suit. You know the one... Yes, it's fantastic... No, no tie. A shimmery black t-shirt... Three dollars from the Salvation Army!... What's that?... Yes, I *am* very Sharon Stone that way... Of course I made the rounds! *I'm* capable of mingling and talking with new people... A lovely fellow named Shaun.... An old friend, Bill, whom I hadn't seen in ages... Yes, of course you know him, I forgot! Oh, I don't know, puppets or something. Oh, and that *divine* William Ivey Long. You know, he dressed me in "Cabaret"... "Undressed" me in "Cabaret"? Well put, my dear, considering those costumes... Yes, of course he *is* doing "that movie". Had just come from his final fitting with Nathan Lane, in fact... Oh, come on, you *know* Nathan and Matthew are doing the film... How's that?... No, I think I'll live without being one of a hundred singing Nazis. . . . Oh, it's *so* true; there's that whole set of chorus boys who can shuttle back and forth between "The Producers" and "Sound of Music." So lucky for them really. Blondes, you know. . . Dinner was fantastic, although I only had a bite or two as we performed afterwards. . . Now, you stop! Only two glasses before the show. . . White. . . Well, yes, we did just have the one dressing room. It was an event facility, after all, not a theater. Most congenial, really. At one point I was brushing my teeth in the john and that lovely Donna Murphy stuck her head in to ask if I had seen her shoes because she had left her underwear in them. . . No, I didn't ask if they were her second pair. None of my business, really, was it?. . . Yes, I *was*! I swear!. . . Briefs. . . White. . . Anyway, I'm sitting there sucking on my reed and who should come through the door but Chita!. . . Yes, she looks amazing. . . I don't know, a hundred at least, I should think. . . Looks fantastic, though. . . Oh, and that girl with the teeth from "Princess Diaries". . . I know, but you should hear her sing! A revelation!. . . Yes, our opening number was sensational. Oh, and just *who* do you think was our Emcee for "Wilkommen"?. . . No, not even warm. . . I had suggested that charming RuPaul, but she hasn't worked with either of the Marshalls. . . Oh, I'll just tell you. *Scott Ellis!. . .* Yes, you *do so* know Scott. He started out as a chorus boy and now he just directs every other show on Broadway... What's that?... "Hope for me yet"? So droll of you, darling. How was that audition, by the way?... No? Pity. Anyway, *Scott*: Well he just directed "12 Angry Men" and "She Loves Me" and "1776" and just about anything else you can think of!... He's a doll. Adorably nervous about performing again but flawless... Yes, it went off without a hitch. Robbie was at the center table with Renee and John C... yes, both from the "Chicago" movie... No, she didn't have that awful black hair like she did at the Oscars... Oh, you're *so* right! Between the hair and the up and down weight she'll be bald and saggy if she's not careful. But *so* precious! I adore her! Really... Well no, you couldn't say I *know* her... Well no, I didn't exactly *meet* her. The crowds and all. I know how that can be so I gave her her space, as they say... Yes, I'm sure she appreciated it... Well, actually, Chita performed "Nowadays"... Unbelievable, I know! One by one she was joined by friends and co-workers of Robbie and Kathleen... Well, Lenora Nemetz for one!... Yes, Lenora!... Looks better than ever. You know the Lenora legend, don't you?... Yes, it *is* true, because she told me herself... No, it wasn't Chita, it was Gwen. Lenora stood by for both of them in the original "Chicago" in '75. During previews Gwen had an injury, but Lenora had never rehearsed... No, not one rehearsal! So Bobby—such a loss!—personally came out on stage before the show and asked the audience to root for her... She was spectacular, of course! Anyway, after that they gave Harvey his award... Droned on and on, as a matter of fact. Not nearly as funny as he is onstage... What?... What's that?... No! Tell me you're joking! Harvey *Weinstein*, not Fierstein?!... The motion picture fellow?... Now that you mention it, they *did* make a couple of Disney jokes I didn't quite get. Well, my dear, that does explain his expression when I told him how much he was missed in "Hairspray"... Now, stop! You're just being mean, now. "I could be a dancer," indeed!... The finale? Charming. *Charming!* The whole lot of us made it to the stage and did the number as if we'd rehearsed for days... Yes, darling, "professional"... Can we *please* not go through that again?... Thank you, dear... Afterwards? Mayhem, just as you'd expect. A little mingling, a little networking. Oh! And I met that queer fellow.... Yes, I know most of them were, but I mean from TV... No, just cable... You know, that show you love... yes, that's it! "Carson", that's his name. So charming, so down to earth. He swears he never goes out, but I've seen him myself about once a week for the past six months... Yes, the entire evening was thrilling and I'm thrilled I was asked... Yes, *totally* exhausted. Oh, hold on darling, can you? I have a

call coming in. I'll be right back... ... ...
Dearest, I *must* run. I completely forgot I'm having lunch with that dreamboat from "42nd Street." No, the *tenor*!... Oh, don't congratulate me *yet*! What?... Oh, yes, *au revoir* to you, too. Oh, how I envy you your French!... Yes, I swear I'll give you *all* the details. Even though you *know* how I hate to talk on the phone... Yes, my dear. Kisses to Derwood! Ciao!

"DID YOU HAVE A VIEW?"

To the far right of the view from my comfortable terrace here at Turtle Cottage on the island of Saba in the Dutch Antilles lies a mountain peak... [totally random aside—that opening line sounded just like Barbara Stanwyck's bogus country life column in "Christmas in Connecticut." You may never know if I'm even really here.) Anyway, about this mountain peak; it's there and it's almost always shrouded in mist. No, not shrouded so much as used as a piece of exercise equipment by the constant fog. The clouds vault over the mountain the same way car commercials used to tout the aerodynamic properties of 1970s gas-guzzlers by shooting a jet of smoke over the contours of a sedan.

This is Mt. Scenery. At 2855 feet it is jokingly (and accurately) referred to as "the highest point in The Netherlands" and hiking to its summit is de rigueur for visitors to Saba. I was a slug on my first visit to the island so I didn't even consider a climb. But this time, with all summer to kill, I had no excuse. Yesterday I decided to make my assault.

The trail up the mountain is an oddity: most of it is either paved with asphalt or has steps cut into the stone, but it's also a non-stop ascent and, because it's a rainforest, the way can be very slick. The humidity encourages lush, oversized vegetation; the trees and rocks wear thick green moss like a gramma with her sweater pulled tight in the air-conditioning.

I had no intention of climbing to the summit in one fell swoop. Along the way there are brief detours to scenic overlooks and—the real point of my hike—a restaurant where I planned to have lunch.

The Ecolodge is just what the name implies: an environmentally-friendly guest house. They use solar power as much as possible, provide no phones or televisions and grow as much of their own produce as they can. They do have hot showers—if it's been sunny enough to heat the water. You can get to the Ecolodge from an access road but the dramatic approach is through the forest. Following the pointer from the main trail you start to notice the flowers along the path gradually becoming more manicured and domesticated. Then you round a bend and the Ecolodge restaurant sits in front of you like a pavilion straight out of the Clark Gable/Jean Harlow movie "Red Dust"; wide verandas and long bands of windows with hurricane shutters propped open for shade. Inside it's cool and dark. And nearly silent. Because there's no music piped in the diners tend to murmur to one another rather than speak at a normal volume. Silverware clinks on china. It's almost eerily quiet.

I imagined I was adventurer in the wild striding in for some drink and conversation; slapping my crop on the bar, my pet monkey climbing down from my shoulders to grab a banana from the bunch hanging by the door; I pull the kerchief from around my neck to wipe my sweaty forehead as I order a rum. From Thomas Mitchell.

In real life I had neither a crop, a monkey nor a kerchief. Or a rum. And the bartender was played by a young blond named Dana who spoke with the same voice and cadence as Shelley Duvall. Dana is married to the son of the founder of Ecolodge and she can really put together a beautiful plate of food. For me, a grilled tuna salad. Talk about your childhood wishes—you can even eat the flowers. After killing some time with my book and an after-meal toothpick, Pogo climbed back on my shoulder as I saluted Dana with my crop and left the restaurant to resume my ascent.

The higher I got, the more lush the vegetation. Snatches of Debussy played in my head that—as I climbed further into the clouds—morphed into Max Steiner jungle drums. Although I wouldn't have been surprised to spot a poorly animated pterodactyl I wasn't expecting the speckled hen that darted across my path with a Bantam rooster in close pursuit. Huh?

The heat, humidity and the cardio workout necessitated frequent rests the further along the trail I got. A pair of hikers came out of the mist on their way down. "Did you have a view" I asked? Nope—just clouds. That's the thing about Mt. Scenery: the clouds that make it so scenic from below tend to make a mockery of its name once you're at the peak.

As the trail finally leveled off I came within yards of the radio tower that sits on top of the mountain. I don't want to think about what went into carting the materials up here to build this behemoth. And from the looks of things, it's not even in operation. The weird orange moss growing everywhere reminded me of the photos of the Titanic at the bottom of the ocean. Corroded cable hung from the structure and huge satellite dishes lay foundering on the rocks at its base. The top of the tower was enveloped in roiling clouds and the constant wind made everything mysterious and spooky. Yes, it was altogether ooky.

I continued past the tower to the summit. There, a huge slab of rock affords a perfect spot to rest and take in the view. When there is one. Yesterday there was nothing but clouds. I stared into the abyss. It was impossible to tell what was past the end of the outcropping: it might have been more rocks or it could have been just a sheer drop to the sea. I kept my distance from the edge.

Since I had no schedule, and to rest up for the equally taxing climb down, I wedged myself into a cleft in the boulder and took out my book, the mist and the wind making it almost chilly. I got through a couple of chapters when I found myself squinting and felt my face turn warm. The sun! I bolted upright and looked out onto an amazing panorama of most of Saba. There, far below me, was the town. To the right, the road to The Bottom. To the left Windwardside and the way down to the airport. Just as I reached into my pack for my camera, the clouds came back and obscured the view. Brigadoon-like, the vista had disappeared into the mists.

But for a brief moment, I had a view.

September 25, 1 A.M.

I'm not really into the miracle thing, okay? I mean, I'm a big ol' atheist and all, so the concept doesn't quite fit into my non-belief system. But I experienced a miracle tonight.

I just finished watching "Angels In America" on DVD. Bruce and I had seen it on Broadway. Neither of us liked it; we thought it was pretentious and silly. And there was enough acting going on up on that stage to fill *three* theaters. When that damn angel broke through the ceiling at the end of Part I it was all we could do to keep from giggling out of control.

So, fast-forward—what—10 years? You can imagine my skepticism upon hearing of the movie version. Yeah yeah yeah Mike Nichols was directing it and it had a cast that really doesn't make sense because, since many of them are big stars, no one could afford them all. I suppose it had everything going for it, but, Bruce and I just hated it so much, how could it possibly be good?

I watched Part I last night and finished it off tonight with Part II.

And it was *so* good. I was practically crying at the opening credits as at the ethereal helicopter shot flying over America on a day when the entire country is experiencing weather from heaven—*from heaven*. At the end of the sequence the camera comes swooping down to the Bethesda Fountain (like the character in the story, one of my favorite spots in Central Park) and the whole movie just got better and better as the hours flew by.

What happened? Is it possible it was the production itself in the 1990s that left us cold? I mean, it's the same story, and, from what I can recall, sticks very close to the original. Was it the acting? The day we saw it? Maybe what Bruce and I had for dinner beforehand stuck in our craw as much as the play. Gosh, it could just have been our seats.

I don't have a theory on this one. I just know that Mike Nichols & Co. performed a bit of alchemy and transformed a piece I thoroughly despised into a long, long movie that moved me tremendously.

Miraculous though? Nah. That ain't no miracle.

The miracle occurred while I was watching the end credits through tear-filled eyes. I've experienced this miracle before, but with decreasing frequency and not for a very long time. It wasn't a long miracle. In fact, it lasted no longer than the time it took for a tiny little electrical charge in my brain that had been tripping along very nicely, thank you, to become distracted by something. A pesky lobe? A sunset over the left hemisphere? Who can say, really? Anyway, this electrical charge became distracted and hopped onto the *wrong neuron!*

And at that instant I thought to myself, "I have to remember to tell Bruce how good this movie was."

And for that miraculously short length of time—so brief that scientists have no unit of measurement for it—Bruce was alive once more.

And that was a miracle.

CICCIOLINA, MISS AMERICA, AND ME

All my life it seems as if I've been running from something; full-time employment, serious relationships, Little League... Once I even ran from a neighbor's goose as it chased me around the yard and up onto the hood of their Chrysler Imperial. So, imagine my surprise, earlier this year, when I found myself running *for* a seat on the Equity Council, the governing body of Actor's Equity.

The "42nd Street" tour I had recently finished was a mixed experience: we had a terrific show with a wonderful cast, yet my salary—as a principal—was one-third of what it had been in the chorus of the National Tour of "Cabaret". The producers and presenting organizations (including Clear Channel, irrefutable proof of the existence of Satan) bore some responsibility, but Equity caved to almost all the demands they were presented with.

I wanted to do everything in my power to see that this situation did not repeat itself. Getting involved in Union activities seemed like a good way to start. But, since leaving the show, I had gone into porn. Wouldn't that complicate a campaign? Or would the membership of Actor's Equity agree that they needed a representative who could not only kick some butt, but who could lick it as well?

Where on Earth could I turn for advice on *that*?

Cicciolina.

Hard-core porn star and Member of Italian Parliament for 15 years. I e-mailed her for advice:

"Would it be possible for you to jot down a few lines telling me how your porn stardom helped (or hurt) when you ran for Parliament? Your insight would be greatly appreciated."

I hit "send" and went back to work on my campaign.

There were three available seats on the council and seven of us on the ballot. If I could make my case and reach enough people, I figured I had a good chance. To that end I prepared an e-mail blitz and set up a webpage detailing my position. Yes, the webpage had a picture on it. I, myself, have voted for Equity Council based solely on candidates' photos. If there's a cute guy on the Council, I helped put him there.

But if, in addition to my mug, I could boast an endorsement from an international porn star-cum-politico, I'd be a cinch. When would I hear from Cicciolina?

Several weeks before the election a meeting of the full council was convened and we candidates were given three minutes in which to read a statement. So, it's come to this, I thought; I'm auditioning for actors.

The room was packed and stuffy when I arrived. Ah, there across the room... an empty seat next to a raven-haired, statuesque beauty. From the way she studied her note pad it was clear she was a fellow candidate. She possessed a certain regal bearing, almost as if... as if there should be a crown on her head. Hold on now, there *was* a crown on her head at one time.

It was Kate Shindle and she was one of our Sally Bowleses in "Cabaret". But, more to the point, she was a former Miss America. No fair! That's sure to sway some voters, I thought. (At least I wasn't running against Vanessa Williams. She'd have had the Miss America thing *and* the porn thing and would have mopped the floor with me.)

I plunked myself down next to Kate and we wished each other luck. Only in the theater would a Miss America and a gay porn star be on the same ballot.

Before the meeting, one of the mucky-mucks from Equity approached me and said he had received an irate, anonymous e-mail saying it was shameful I was allowed to run. "Don't worry about it," he said. "I looked at your site. I enjoyed your, uh, *writing*."

Hmmm. . . the only reason I hadn't been riding on Gus's coattails was that I didn't think it would be right to campaign with an unfair advantage. Was I letting a great marketing ploy slip through my fingers? I thought it best that I let my record speak for itself.

From the road I had written a "report" on our lousy contract. It had spread like wildfire throughout the union, so my bona fides were in order, as far as my commitment to the cause went, and my name was out there as an activist. In the process I had also done a nifty job of blacklisting myself. I became known as the Norma Rae of the company and if I never work again I won't have to wonder why.

From that experience, however, I knew that e-mail was a powerful tool for reaching lots of folks I didn't even know. I sent out a notice announcing my candidacy and waited for the responses to pour in. People wrote saying they remembered my report and would vote for me. I was starting to let myself become cautiously optimistic.

But, still no word from Italy. Where were my pearls of wisdom; my words of encouragement? Where was the quote for my webpage?

After a second round of e-mail campaigning I received a note from a stranger saying, "I don't know how you are as an actor, but you're a helluva campaigner."

Things were looking good.

As it happened, the day the ballots were counted I was on location north of San Francisco shooting a video. Someone from Equity would be calling with the results and I imagined being borne shoulder-high around the set after receiving the good news while Chi Chi playfully squirted me with lube and my costars presented me with a bouquet of condoms.

It was a tough B-Roll shoot that day, and I had forgotten about the election when, during a break, I checked my messages.

"Hello, this is Actor's Equity calling with the election results. . . "

"Sshhhh! Quiet everybody. I think this is it!", I hissed.

The voice continued: "We're sorry to inform you that you did not. . . "

I gently closed my phone and stuck it in my bag.

I finished the day sporting a stiff upper lip (among other things) and rode silently back to the motel in the back of the van. After a shower I logged on to check my e-mail and, at last , there it was in my inbox:

"Caro Gus,

I hope you yet visitation my beautiful official site where you can find and buy my beautiful book "Memorie" a colours of 192 pg. (photographer a colours) where you find any response for your many questions. . .

Big Kisses"

That was it? "Big kisses" and a pitch for her book? She didn't even sign her name.

Later I learned that the meager 20% of the union membership who voted simply re-instated incumbent members. I came in 4th out of seven; Kate one from the bottom (I guess Atlantic City just ain't Broadway.) It's a shame, because she's well-spoken and committed.

Since the election, I've made a bunch of dirty movies, Kate's playing Sally Bowles somewhere in Westchester County, and Cicciolina? Well, she's selling her beautiful book online.

Losing my bid for Equity Council, combined with my twin losses at the GayVNs and Grabbys, proved to be discouraging, although it didn't shake my conviction that I can lick butt better than any of those damned incumbents.

But you can be sure that next time I run for something, it'll be a bus.

COME OUT, COME OUT WHEREVER YOU ARE

A little-reported subplot in the recent resignation of New Jersey Governor James McGreevey is that persistent rumors regarding his homosexuality had been circulating since he assumed office. In other words, everyone already knew.

This is my case—inspired by several moving e-mails I have received from visitors to this site—for proudly stating (as Jim McGreevey did) that "I am a gay American." As he said, coming out to the world will, "keep me from the pitfalls of a divided self or secret truths."

Those "secret truths" are usually very open secrets; they're the proverbial elephant in the room that goes unmentioned. But, by leaving things undefined, by not being clear about one's relationship to the world vis-á-vis one's sexuality, not only are those who would oppress us free to do so with impunity, those who love us are unable to fully share in our lives.

Dick Cheney supports gay marriage.

The one and only reason he arrived at that position is because his daughter is a lesbian. Polls have continuously shown that people who know homosexuals personally are more supportive of gay rights. Here's a news flash for you: *everyone* knows a homosexual. They may not know they do, but I believe it's more likely they've never had to deal with the obvious fact because the person in question has let them off the hook by remaining in the closet.

Therefore, by extrapolation, coming out helps not only the person making the announcement, but the gay population at large. Social policy is formed slowly, over time, as mores and beliefs evolve. Each man and woman who tells their loved ones "I'm gay" is helping to change the minds of six, eight, 10 other people directly and scores of others down the line. It's not too farfetched to say that someone who comes out tomorrow is directly responsible for increasing the likelihood that gay marriage will be fully accepted in the future.

Your friends and family will appreciate it.

When a friend or relative or coworker is still in the closet, there tends to be a lot of acrobatic conversational skills in play. So much has to be talked around or ignored.

I'm not blind to the fact that some circumstances might make this task more challenging than others. In some parts of the country it is still pretty tough—if not outright dangerous—to be openly gay. Discretion and subtlety might be more suitable in these situations: why don't you give your best girlfriend at the office an opening (and you know you have a best a girlfriend at the office) and casually mention that you can't wait to see "Ocean's Twelve" because you "think George Clooney is *so* handsome." She'll probably sigh and think to herself, "at last!"

People are fairly intuitive when it comes to those they love. The denial comes into play on the part of the closeted person. A friend of mine lived with his "roommate" in a beautifully decorated house with three Jack Russell Terriers and thought no one had a clue he was gay. I'll wager even the dogs knew.

Because everyone already knows.

Your sister knows. Your father knows (although he's running a close second in the denial department.) Brandy, the checkout girl down at the Piggly Wiggly knows. (Mike the bag boy *hopes* you're gay, but, at 15, he's not yet quite sure why he hopes that.)

Your business associates know.

A producer friend who came out late in life made a big production of taking his colleagues out to dinner—one at a time—to tell them what they had known for years. One actress breathed a sigh of relief and said, "Is *that* all? I was terrified you were going to ask me to do the revival of *Annie 2*!"

In my own case, my mother finally got fed up and said to me, "Tell me, because I know." (Mom also confessed she knew I was gay when I was a baby. If she had any lingering doubts they were fully dispelled when, at age 13, I created a six-foot-long facsimile of Barbra Streisand's signature—resplendent with silver glitter—on the wall of my bedroom.) We were then able to have a conversation without having to think about every word we said and were free to indulge in our normal Presbyterian hang-ups.

But, there's one overwhelming, foudroyant reason for coming out, and it doesn't involve your family and friends. It's not about taking a political stance or moving the gay agenda forward. The best reason for coming out is this: *it is going to make you happy*. You will suddenly find that you've been unknowingly carrying an onerous and debilitating burden. This weight has been keeping your shoulders hunched and your arms at your sides when they could be spread wide as wings, allowing you to soar through your life, concealing nothing, no longer Earth-bound by "secret truths".

When the Munchkins came out from wherever they were they discovered they had been liberated from a life of hiding and fear. Do yourself a favor:

take Glinda's advice. It got Dorothy home safe and it can get you there, too.

NORMAN RAE

Shouldn't there be a union for guys in porn? I'm asked that question often. I understand the logic behind this and, as an insider, appreciate it even more than the porn-buying public at large. What's more, I *am* a union man: I'm a dues-paying member of Actors' Equity Association, the professional actors' union. I've been active in union politics and served as a self appointed bur-under-the-saddle of the producers of the National Tour of "42nd Street" a few years back when we were hampered with a sub-standard contract.

Bear all that in mind when I repeat my answer to the above-mentioned query: It ain't gonna fly.

Labor is organized for two main purposes: to achieve fair wages for members' efforts and to promote healthy and safe working conditions. Let's address the second point first. Just what constitutes safe working conditions in an industry that is based around men having sex with other men? Mandatory condom usage? That's already in place at all the mainstream studios. The barebacking fringe companies obviously would never agree to such demands. Guys that appear in bareback videos are pretty much blacklisted from the big studios. Let's face it; the only foolproof way to ensure safe conditions on a porn set is to prohibit the sex. In the theater the actual performing surface is an issue in all contracts. Do you even want to think about the "performing surface" at the end of a video shoot? I don't think so.

But it's wages most people mean when they bring up the idea of a union. I wouldn't know where to begin to set a fair *per scene* rate for a video shoot. (That's how we're paid in porn, incidentally; per scene.) What if the performer appears in a solo jackoff scene? Or is in the background in a large orgy? How about if a two-way evolves into a larger group after the initial cumshots? Should the first couple get paid for one or for two scenes? And what if a guy is unable to cum? Should there be a penalty? Or is there a bonus if he comes twice? What about minimum erection duration? Is a bottom more valuable than a top or vice versa? And what about workhorses like me who get saddled with lots of dialogue ("B-roll", as it's quaintly referred to in the industry) for no additional compensation? Should I go on strike? All by myself?

Which artfully brings us to the next point: A union of less than all possible talent is toothless. Collective bargaining can only work if the entire workforce is committed to the idea and willing to forego employment knowing that it will strengthen the union. Forming a Porn Actors' Guild, like any other union, would entail initial drawbacks and monetary loss. Corporations don't like unions. (Perhaps you've heard the name Wal-Mart?) They have to be wrassled to the ground to agree to an organized workforce. That means all of the guys making porn, and all the guys who are *thinking* about making porn, would have to decline movie gigs in the short-term until the studios had no choice but to hire union performers.

And here we have the crux of the matter. In porn, "short-term" is the only term there is. Men going into porn don't think about it as a lifelong career. There are a very few cases where performers' careers have lasted a decade or more, but you can count them on one hand. Most young men (and they *are* mostly young) aren't thinking past the end of the day, much less 5 or 6 years down the road. Will they be willing to part with $500 of their $1000 fee for union initiation if they think this movie will be their first and last?

In 1913 New York actors shut down Broadway with a strike and forced the producers to the bargaining table. In 2003 one of the major issues confronting the 90-year-old union was the willingness of young performers to accept non-union employment. And that's a business in which people hope to spend their entire lives. One afternoon on a porn set—as a lark—doesn't engender commitment to "the cause."

I'm no apologist for the porn industry. Do I think we performers are treated fairly by the production companies? No. Do I think the studios are making profits way out of proportion to what we're paid? Yes, I do. Do I think we should earn residuals on the units sold? You bet. But there is no single performer in the business that could not be replaced with someone equally as popular, so holding out for a cut would be meaningless. When I was working regularly in porn was there anyone holding a gun to my head? Not that I ever noticed.

Don't get me wrong, I believe the biggest dilemma facing the heads of the various production companies—several of whom are friends, I hasten to add—is how to spend their excess profits. And I do feel that the naïvete of vulnerable young men is exploited by those same companies. (If I were in charge of this hypothetical union, 30 would be the minimum age to be eligible to work.) But since I am congenitally unable to hold a job for any length of time I have work experience in many disparate fields and can say without hesitation that there is virtually nothing unique about the porn business.

Except that it can't be organized.

THE HOUSE PAINTER

Climbing the sidewalk up the hill from the train, Clive Simmons managed to convey a sense of dignity despite the circumstances in which he found himself. The elbows and knees of his tweed suit were worn, but the suit itself was clean. With his thin, elegant moustache and slight British accent he managed to present a picture of someone who had not been as deeply affected by the Depression as, in fact, he had. Prosperity might be around the corner, as the last President had said, but Clive had never had a good sense of direction. So, he was glad to have the address—engraved just beneath "Mrs. Marion Giles, Rooms"—on the card he held in his hand.

Six months in New York after returning from his studies in France had left him near penniless. Evenings in his sweltering flat were spent anointing canvas after canvas with oil paints—tubes of color that were becoming more 180precious in direct proportion to his decreasing funds. His *maitre* in Paris had encouraged him in his visual experiment; Clive was trying to perfect the technique of seamlessly blending colors from opposite sides of the spectrum into one another.

He hoped to reach the point where the viewer's eye would discern cobalt blue, then cadmium orange then manganese violet before realizing the hue had completely changed. His work progressed through autumn and continued even now when the early winter cold made his fingers stiff as he stood at his easel. But, the matter of rent was quickly overriding artistic pursuit.

Packing a small bag, along with his paint box and a few canvasses, he took the Hudson River Tubes to Hoboken and there boarded a northbound train. The Simmonses had left Monroe years earlier, but it was an area Clive knew well and, at this point, familiarity would be as welcome as friendship. And a man he had met at the artist's supply store had given him the business card of a young widow with inexpensive, clean rooms to let.

Mrs. Giles's house was a two-storey affair with a wide front porch. It sat on the street among similar houses. The shade offered by the enormous maples must be welcome in summer, thought Clive, but now, under the gray November sky, they served merely as a skeletal reminder of warmer days.

The shingles of the house were painted white on the second floor and green—Forest green, he'd have to say—at street level, thereby distinguishing it from the solid-color dwellings on either side. There was one area at the back of the house near the kitchen door, however, that was still the old brown. Mr. Giles had gotten just this far with the project when his wife, Marion, found him hanging from a rope around his neck in the detached garage. Month after month of a fruitless search for employment had taken its irreversible toll on the man, leaving his young wife to fend for herself. Two years later the brown patch remained as a silent testament to continuing hard times.

Responding to the knock at the front door, Marion emerged from her kitchen wiping her hands on a towel. Her chintz dress complemented her black hair, which, in turn, drew attention away from the fact that, really, the dress was quite threadbare and faded.

"Mrs. Giles," asked Clive. Marion reacted to his dapper appearance by instinctively reaching up a hand to smooth the hair piled on her head.

"Yes?"

"You received my telegram saying I would arrive today?"

"Oh, Mr. Simmons, of course," replied Marion, opening the screen door to her newest paying guest, the relief in her eyes momentarily erasing the tired sadness that usually showed there. "Please come in out of the cold. I just put a tray of biscuits in the oven for dinner. Why don't I show you your room and I'll bring some into the front parlor."

The small china plate sat on the table between them, a few stray crumbs sitting amid a pool of honey that had dripped off the warm, flaky buns. Clive agreed, yes, it was nice of her friend, Mr. Clark, to give him Marion's card. No, he did not know Mr. Clark very well. Would Mrs. Giles object to Clive setting up his easel in his room. Of course, he would be very careful with the paints and the solvents.

"Well, I don't really know. . . Would you be able to work in the garage? There's a stove there. I don't use it for anything, uh, anymore."

"Yes, Mr. Clark explained that to me. That would be fine, thank you. I would like to pay you two weeks' rent in advance." Marion thanked Clive and watched as he climbed the stairs to his room.

During the following weeks leading up to the holidays, Clive and Marion became more comfortable with each other. Marion had no interest in art or in travel, but she enjoyed listening to Clive talk about things even if she didn't understand them. And Clive appreciated the company. Marion didn't quite understand what he was attempting to do with his shading colors, but she was sure it would be lovely, just lovely.

Clive spent most mornings in his studio garage, stopping to rub his fingers in front of the small coal stove when the cold became more intense. Marion wouldn't come into to the garage, but she'd call to him from the kitchen door if something was warm just out of the oven.

Clive would come in to the house, passing the patch of brown near the kitchen door, and the two of them would spend a few moments together before returning to their work. Sometimes Clive would borrow a bowl or some fruit to to use as a subject. Marion was reluctant to let him take the vase of Cala Lilies her sister had brought her, but Clive made her see how perfect they would be t paint. She was disappointed later when he failed to bring them back into the house.

One afternoon, after replacing the blue enameled coffee pot on the stove, Marion sat at the table across from Clive and, screwing up her courage, said, "I hope you don't mind, but, since you do owe two weeks' room and board, I asked at the new school up the street and, well, they're ready to work on the interior and all the classrooms need to be painted, and. . . " Her voice trailed off as she saw Clive's posture stiffen.

"Oh, yes," said Clive, sounding slightly more British than usual, "while I do understand the position I have placed you in, I hope you will appreciate that I am not a house painter."

"Yes, but . . . "

"Thank you for the pie. I really should return to my work."

Flushed, Marion blurted out, "You will be joining us for Thanksgiving on Thursday, I hope." Clive replied, "Thank you, I'll be sure to let you know if I can," and closed the kitchen door behind him, walking slowly back to his studio, past the brown patch on the side of the house.

The next few days were as chilly inside as they were outdoors in the steely November cold. Clive stayed in the garage until late at night, painting, and Marion fixed him a tray in his room for supper. That Wednesday, as he headed upstairs, he found a telegram placed just outside his room. He picked it up and went inside, closing the door behind him.

Marion was up early the following morning, her younger sister having come by before the rest of the family to help with the Thanksgiving meal. Looking at the clock above the stove she realized that Clive was sleeping much later than he usually did. She climbed the stairs and stood in the hallway outside his room, listening for sounds of life on the other side of the door. Hearing nothing but the tick of the clock on the landing, she knocked gently.

"Mr. Simmons? I thought you might want to know what time it is so you could get ready to join us for dinner." She opened the door a crack and looked in the room. The bed was neatly made and Clive's suitcase, which usually sat on the stand at under the window, was gone. Marion walked stonily down to the kitchen, torn between anger and disappointment.

Ignoring her sister's queries she stalked across the yard to the garage, the dead, brown grass crunching under her low-heeled shoes with each determined step. Along with repeated cries of, "Mr. Simmons!" she knocked firmly on the garage door. But, still there was no response.

Marion took a deep breath and pulled open the heavy garage door. She stepped into the gloom; the dust stirred by her footsteps dancing lazily in the shafts of sunlight coming in through the two eight-paned windows on the wide door. She had not been in here since her husband's death two years ago and, even now, lowered her gaze so she would not see the beam above her head that had played a leading role in the turn her life had taken.

As her eyes became accustomed to the darkness, Marion could just make out an artist's easel standing at the far side of the room near the cold stove. Walking towards it she knocked into a small table, just managing to catch the vase it held before it fell to the dirt floor. As she got closer she realized she was looking at the back of the easel. There was a canvas mounted on it, and a note was tacked to the frame of the canvas. She took the note and, holding it at an angle in a shaft of sunlight, read its contents:

"Dear Mrs. Giles,

Our friend Mr. Clark has come through once again. He has secured me a position on a Federal arts project. I will be working with a crew of fellow artists painting murals in a new Library in Ohio. While I am afraid I cannot pay you the rent I owe you, I hope you will accept this picture in lieu of payment. Thank you for all your kindness.

Sincerely,

Clive Simmons

P.S Please forgive my taking the liberty of finishing the job."

The only word that came to her mind was "miffed". She was *miffed* at the audacity of this man. She wondered what Mr. Simmons expected her to pay *her* bills with. And, what could he possibly mean by "finishing the job"?

Circling around to the front of the easel, she saw a small, narrow canvas, on which was painted five white Cala Lillies. They were beautiful. Even more beautiful than the real ones her sister had brought her. But, it was the background of the painting that caused Marion to stare. The lilies were not positioned in a vase, nor were they arranged against any recognizable background. They were simply floating above color. Three colors, in fact. The background faded from blue to rose to black, but it was impossible to tell where one color ended and the next began.

So, this was what Clive had been trying to explain to her. It was so clear, once she saw the results.

Marion took the canvas from the easel and left the garage, closing the door behind her, for the first time not thinking about what had happened inside. She held the painting carefully in front of her and looked at it as she walked back towards the house. She raised her eyes as she neared the kitchen door and let out a small gasp. The arm holding the painting slowly fell to her side and she raised her other hand and cupped it over her open mouth. Looking straight ahead she saw that the patch of brown next to the kitchen door was gone, covered over by a fresh coat of green.

Forest green, she would have to say.

Clive Simmons was never heard from again. But, Marion's younger sister was my grandmother and the painting of five Cala Lilies he left behind that cold Thanksgiving morning hangs on the wall in front of me—just to the left of the window—as I sit writing these words.

PANHANDLE MANHANDLE

Mrs. Dahlia Strunk, hostess, Brass Buckle Family Restaurant:

"Well, course I remember him comin' in here. On account it was Mother's Day, which, as you know, is our busiest day of the year. Folks'd be makin' their reservations startin' right after President's Day sometimes. Honestly, I wisht one of these years the families would decide to *cook* for the mothers 'stead of taking 'em out. It just seems to me that.... What? Oh, all right. It was a Sunday—goes without saying—and, well, we was packed. Hot, too. This part of Oklahoma heats up pretty early, y'know? That reservation book was full-up weeks before. Which really ain't surprising, because we *are* the best restaurant in the Panhandle. I had just seated the Preebo family (Lord, you should see that oldest gal—must tip the scales at 200 pounds if she's an ounce) and Charlene here—Charlene, you spit that gum out *pronto!* 'fore I stick it behind your ear. And answer that damn phone—comes up and says can I seat a single. A *single*, I tell her! I say, girl that peroxide musta gone to your brain, I can't seat no single on

Mother's Day, just look at this place. Well, Charlene looks at me with those big cow eyes of hers and I can tell she feels sorry for this fella, being by hisself on Mother's Day. So, I squeezed him in over there on 9A—that deuce over there by the beverage station. He didn't stay long, but I heard he left a nice tip. No, I can't really recall anything else in particular. What's that Charlene? Oh, that's right! No, *I'll* tell it! Get this—he just ate a bunch of vegetables. Was one of them vegetarians, I suppose. Now, I ask you; what the hell is the point in that? I always say, "If God didn't want us to eat no animals, he wouldn't-a made 'em out of meat!" He was real friendly-like on his way out. Gave me a compliment on my hairdo, can you imagine? Said he had a long drive in front of him. What's that? No, sir, I never would-a guessed that boy would get hisself involved with the law. Oh, and mister, 'Hostess' up there at the top needs a capital H on it."

Mr. Burt Hendricks and Mr. Morris "Stewy" Jankowski, retired:

"I don't mind telling you me and Burt are kind of proud of ourselves for how that all turned out. Ain't we, Burt?"

"You ain't lyin', mister."

"Well, Burt and me come down to the Wal-Mart on account of it was Mother's Day and I was picking up somethin' special for the Missus."

"How much did that leaf-blower set you back, Stewy?"

"That thing was on sale pretty nice. You shoulda seen Edna's face when I came in after the V.F.W. and told her what I had just set in the garage for her."

"She liked it, did she?"

"Who wouldn't? So, there's Burt and me in the parking lot out in front of the Wal-Mart and Burt says to me, 'Would you look at that, Stewy? That there looks like an old Ford Falcon.'"

"You ain't lyin' 'bout that! And then you let out that low whistle like you do and said we oughta go over there and see that sweet old thing."

"So, Burt and me goes over to the car and I see it has New York plates on it."

"That was our first clue."

"Well, sir, there's this feller sittin' in the driver's seat lookin' through a whaddayacallit, a knapsack. . . "

"Lookin' hard for somethin'. . . "

"And so I says to him, 'That's quite a sweet car you're drivin' there, mister. That's a '63, ain't it?' and he looks up at us and says, 'Actually, it's a '61. You can tell by the turn signals in the grille.' Kinda snooty, if you want my opinion."

"He said that like he was used to answerin' that question, somehow. Said he was drivin' all the way to California. Got all this way without any kind of car trouble."

"Burt and me started askin' him about his car. That fool New Yorker didn't even know what kinda engine was in it. You thought that was odd, didn't you, Burt?"

"I think he mighta been one of them 'funny fellas', y'know? You think so, Stewy?"

"All I know is he was bent on finding something and he was looking everywhere. We followed him around the back of his car when he went lookin' in the trunk and, well, that's when we saw 'em. Sittin' right on top there like he was, well, like he was *proud* to show 'em off or somethin'. Disgusting, if you ask me."

"You ain't lyin' about that! A bag full of drugs."

"Big ol' bag full of drugs. Huh? No, sir, I couldn't tell you what kind, but I guess I know drugs when I see 'em."

"Sittin' right there on top of his suitcase. Pills like you ain't never seen. Buncha different colors and everythin'.

"Damn liberal New Yorkers think they can just come out here and push their drugs. Yeah, well, when that damn liberal New Yorker said somethin' about having to call his sister. . . "

"Bet that damn liberal don't even have no sister..."

"...well, that's when Burt and me called the Highway Patrol. Yessiree, just called right on over there to Guymon and reported that damn Jew druggie."

"Stewy's a good American that way."

"Bob Young's boy picked him up later on. Woulda got clean away if I hadn't called it in."

"Yup, a good American."

"Nope, never did hear what happened to him. Yeah, well, Burt and me gotta get goin'. There's some kind of meeting down at the V.F.W. we gotta get to."

"You ain't lyin' 'bout that, Stewy. No sir."

Bud Grimsby, greeter:
"Hello welcome to Wal-Mart do you need a cart"

Meghan O'Flynn-Steinman, attorney (non-practicing):
"Well, yeah, I did think it was odd when I spotted him in that field. Especially in the Oklahoma panhandle. Although, after this trip I'm redefining my standard for 'odd'. Leonard—Leonard Steinman, my husband—thought it would be this great idea for the whole family to drive cross-country to visit his mother. 'Cross-country?' You do that on skis, I said, not in a minivan with three

kids and a dog! Sure, he goes into the city to the firm every day in his nice, cushy Lexus and thinks this is some kind of a treat or something. Well, let's just say Leonard may be redefining 'treat' after this trip. I mean, up to St. Louis you could at least eat half-way decently, but just try to find something on the menus here that's not fried or smothered in cheese. They even have fried cheese! And, can someone please explain to me when marshmallows became a salad ingredient? We ate at some dump where the hostess had, like, green teeth and this hideous bouffant. Don't even get me started about the clothes. Jesus God! Here it was Mother's day and the kids wanted to get me something. 'There's Wal-Mart', they screamed. 'And here's the Nieman-Marcus catalog', I said and threw it into the back seat. 'Circle something and give it back to your father.' Yeah, so, we're driving on this boring, flat road through this boring, flat state on this boring, hot day in this smelly car on the way to California to see Letty Steinman (absolutely my most favorite person in the entire frigging world) and Sean—the oldest—says, 'What's that guy doing?' 'What guy? There's no guy, Sean.' And, then all the kids start screaming like they're on fire or something (which, let me tell you, is a distinct possibility at this point if they're not careful) and pointing into the field. Well, there's this guy walking around some kind of junkyard. But, it's not cars in the junkyard, it's, uh, trailers or something. Y'know, like in a trailer park. Old, rusty things. Crap, if you ask me. But, he's taking pictures of all this stuff, and his car—which looks like a piece of junk itself—is parked by the side of the road. It all seemed damned suspicious to me. 'Maybe we should tell somebody,' Leonard says. Very calmly I said, 'Leonard, what does the fuel gauge say?... That's right, full. Now, let me make myself clear—you're not taking your goddam foot off that goddam gas pedal until we cross the state line and get out of this fucking state!' Yes, Sean, Mommy said the f-word. Just deal with it. God dammit, would you all stop screaming! Oh, my god, I need another... Sean, hand me my purse. Now!"

Mike Young, Oklahoma Highway Patrol:

"I got word from dispatch at approximately 1:20 PM that a white male, apparently early thirties, was suspected of transporting drugs in his vehicle. Suspect was headed west on Route 64 and was driving a black 1961 Ford Falcon, New York tags. Apparently the call came in to headquarters from old Stewy Jankowski, who thinks of himself as some kind of deputy. Normally we wouldn't put too much stock in a call from Stewy, but Burt Hendricks backed up his story so H.Q. figured we oughta take a look. I didn't imagine he would be too difficult to spot. Heck, traffic is so light in this part of the Panhandle he'd like as not be the only car on the road. Sure enough, I saw him coming the opposite direction and made a U-turn and pulled him over. He expressed surprise when informed that his headlight was out, saying he had just replaced it the day before. I asked him to get out of the vehicle and the suspect complied politely. To be honest, I have to say he exhibited a friendly respect throughout the investigation. Well, until Patrolman Steeves showed up, anyway. When Mr. Judson—that was his name, Judson— walked to the front of the car and saw his headlight was functioning properly I informed him of the actual reason for pulling him over. He sort of stammered and appeared a little flustered at first, but when I asked his permission to frisk him he calmed down some. It has been my experience that most people seem to tense up when they're frisked, but Mr. Judson didn't seem to have a problem with it. I asked his permission to search his vehicle (and assured him, no, it wouldn't be necessary to do a strip-search) and he immediately assented to the request. 'Sure, go ahead, I know I don't have anything,' he said as I looked under the seats and in the glove compartment. I was surprised to learn he was driving cross-country in this particular vehicle, but he said he had had no problems up to this point.

Normally I don't converse much during a search, but, as I mentioned, he seemed friendly and like he wasn't hiding anything. He was sort of thinking out loud wondering how the claim against him might have been filed when he said, 'A-ha! I know what it is you're looking for.' He really said 'A-ha,' like in a book or something. He then took me around the rear of the vehicle and opened the trunk. Sitting on top of his luggage was a large Zip-loc bag containing a variety of pills. He said, 'Vitamins. Just a bunch of vitamins and supplements.' He said he figured this was easier than carrying around a bunch of bottles. He guessed that was what Stewy took to be drugs. He was looking for his address book to get his sister's number to call her for Mother's Day when Stewy and Burt were hanging around. After a brief search of the trunk I called in a report to H.Q. and got word back that Patrolman Steeves would come to meet us with the drug-testing kit which would determine the nature of these pills. Being as the day was extremely hot, and Steeves was clear across the county when he called, I invited Tom, uh, Mr. Judson to wait with me in the patrol car. Y'see, his vehicle had no air conditioning. I was fairly certain his story was true, because if you're guilty you're gonna be a little nervous in a patrol car, but Tom seemed right at ease. He was telling me about his drive from New York and asking me questions about

Oklahoma and about my job—he seemed especially interested in the official Highway Patrol uniform. I asked him if some of those supplements were for bodybuilding, 'cause I work out pretty hard myself, and he seemed pretty happy to talk about all that. Said he could sure take some pointers from me, which I took as a compliment, for sure. I admit I was kinda surprised to find out he was almost 10 years older than me. I asked him if he had been through Louisville on his way out, 'cause Diane—that's my fiancée—she's probably gonna be moving there for work. Tom sure thought it was cool when I told him Diane's a jockey! Don't know why that tickled him so much. Maybe he likes horses or something, I dunno. Anyway, Tom and I were comparing our leg routines when Fordy Steeves pulled up. . . "

Medford Steeves, Oklahoma Highway Patrol:

"2:28 P.M. I make visual contact with Patrolman Young's vehicle, which is stationed in front of suspect's vehicle. I am initially surprised to see suspect in passenger seat of P'man Young's vehicle. I discuss situation with P'man Young and determine suspect is unarmed and not dangerous. Suspect attempts to converse but is rebuffed. P'man Young and I confer re. bag of pills. Initial conclusion supports suspect's claim that pills are vitamins, but I test them to be sure. Test confirms pills are vitamins. Based on witnesses' claim of seeing drugs, I determine suspect's vehicle should be searched more thoroughly. When I remove rear seat suspect becomes somewhat agitated (moreso when I enlarge tear in headliner for visual confirmation.) I replace rear seat—no, sir, not because suspect insisted, because I desired to leave suspect with a good impression of the Oklahoma Highway Patrol—and told suspect he was free to go. As I pull away I see suspect exchange words with P'man Young who then signals 'all clear' as suspect continues west on Route 64 toward the state line."

Diane Haverford, jockey:

"I don't know, maybe Mike's just needs a break. First he tells me he's not sure he wants to get married at all right now. I mean, I already told *everyone*. But, then he asks me if there are any good race tracks in California—San Francisco—because he thinks maybe he'd like to move out there. Oh—and this is weird—he wanted to know if I mind if he wears his uniform around the house. I think maybe I'm having second thoughts about all this myself. I was telling my girlfriend Andi about it, and she thinks I should wait; that I could just move in with her. Maybe she's right. I don't know..."

Bud Grimsby, greeter:

"Goodbye thank you for shopping at Wal-Mart have a nice day."

RATTLESNAKES HAVE BEEN OBSERVED

Since the dawn of man, homo sapiens have derived comfort from seasonal milestones. These events help maintain a cyclical sense of continuity that tells us no matter what cataclysmic turns may befall us, the world as we know it will carry on.

Autumn has a particularly abundant selection of such occurrences. Rural folk look to the first frost to delineate one season from the last. Thick, hardy vines, which the day before trailed sturdily among the pumpkins and squash, lie watery and withered on the soil, itself now redolent of seasonal decay. City people watch for fur coats to sprout among the shoppers and business people hurrying along the broad avenues, their shadows growing longer daily as the sun struggles vainly to reach its proud heights of June and July.

For me, fall is heralded by the arrival on store shelves of the first bags of candy corn. These bite-sized confections—known technically as melocremes—state, by their very presence,

"There's no turning back: ready or not, here comes fall."

Each year I consume vast quantities of the stuff. But, perhaps, never as much as on a 10-day driving trip my husband Bruce and I took through Montana in the early 1990s. I need snacks on a long drive. Especially ones that will satisfy my insatiable sweet tooth. And, since this was The Year of Losing Weight, those snacks had to be fat-free, a characteristic that, happily, candy corn possesses.

The previous December, after bidding our final Christmas party guest farewell, Bruce leaned over me as I slouched in the big comfy chair, chin on my chest, covered in cookie crumbs. "Honey, you're really gaining a lot of weight," he said, clearly fearing the argument that was to come. I just laughed. He was right, after all. True love (and pints of Häagen-Dazs every night) will do that. So under the tree that Christmas Bruce found a gift certificate for "One Thinner Husband". I was very clear that it didn't have to be me. Six months and 50 pounds later, Bruce, deciding a tune-up was better than a trade-in, redeemed the certificate for little(r) old me.

Sitting in the passenger seat, my feet up on the dashboard, I could shove fistfuls of candy corn into my mouth with impunity as we drove across Montana. Bruce and I would sing along to the oldies station on the radio and when we stopped to pee by the side of the road, we got a kick of a sign that read, "Rattlesnakes Have Been Observed". The passive voice gave the warning a half-hearted feel that made the serpentine menaces seem almost benign. I pictured the maraca-playing animated snake from the credits of "The Lady Eve" waiting patiently by the side of the road to welcome visitors to The Treasure State.

We were thrilled the first time we crossed the Continental Divide and, by the twentieth time we crossed that demarcation, we'd scream out the window, "Who cares?!" We went on hikes, praying we'd see a bear, only to run like girls when we rounded a corner and found a buffalo sleeping in the sun. We rented a cabin on a lake and dined al fresco as the sun fell lazily behind a snow-capped mountain across the water. And we hiked into Glacier Park, where winter had leap-frogged fall and made us glad we had brought our heavy coats and warm hats.

But, most of all we laughed. And laughed and laughed. These were ten days in our marriage after I was fat and before Bruce was sick and it was a time I will forever use as the standard by which I judge "happy".

We returned to New York to find summer was still very much in evidence; that relatively-temperate island has a way of holding on until the last possible moment. But I had half a bag of candy corn left from the trip, which proved the season really was about to change.

Bruce had to work the day after we flew home and blew me a kiss from the bedroom door on his way out. As I dragged my sleepy, unemployed butt into the kitchen to start the coffee, I saw that on the kitchen table, spelled out in letters of orange, yellow and white candy corn were eight letters:

I L-O-V-E Y-O-U.

And, so, every year towards the end of September, as my teeth sink into the crystallized outer shell of the season's first striated melocreme, I hop into my confectionary Time Machine and find myself whisked back to ten happy days in Montana. There the sky is always big, the candy corn crop is plentiful and, from time to time, rattlesnakes have been observed.

We Shall Come Rejoicing

While out driving the other day I passed a farmer mowing the hay in his field. Mounted on the side of the tractor was a contraption that pivots to stand upright for transport or lowers flat, perpendicular to the tractor, to cut the hay. It consists of two rows of teeth that shuttle back and forth. Basically, it works on the same principle as an electric carving knife, albeit one of Jurassic proportions.

Once the hay is cut it must dry in the field for a few days before it can be raked and baled. Green (or wet) hay can spontaneously combust in the barn, and that's not particularly desirable among farmers.

How do I know this arcane agrariana? Growing up, our house sat on the corner of my paternal grandparents' dairy farm and bringing in the hay was one of the seasonal chores that the grandsons helped with. There are several cuttings during the growing season, but I remember helping only during July and August. I suppose I was in school the other times.

At 200 acres our family farm was small, and provided a mean existence for my grandparents. There were no hired hands, so the labors of us kids were essential to making sure the lofts were filled to feed the cows during the frigid northeast winters.

Cutting and raking are one-man jobs, done with a tractor and a machine, so I rarely came on the scene until it was time to bale the hay and take it to the barn. Pa drove the green John Deere tractor, which towed the bailing machine (in my mind's eye it's red, which would have made it a McCormick), which, in turn, pulled the hay wagon. That's where my cousins and I were stationed.

On our farm we made rectangular bales; not the round behemoths seen nowadays. The lines of raked hay were fed into the bailer where the hay was formed into bales and tied with twine. From there, the bales came shooting out of the machine—high into the air, like human cannonballs at the circus—to land with a thud on the floor of the hay wagon. Presuming none of us got in the path of the oncoming projectiles, the bales were dragged to the back of the wagon and stacked neatly in rows. This continued until the floor of the wagon was covered, and then still longer until the piled rows of hay bales towered high above the ground, held in place only by a rear support and the ingenuity of the stacking system.

As our convoy bumped and jostled its way back and forth through the field under the baking July sun, it occasionally roused a spray of grasshoppers from their resting place in the hay rows. Bob-whites would complain and scurry as the cacophonous caravan came near, and once I recall a pheasant scolding us as we approached her nest.

We boys had an enormous mayonnaise jar filled with iced-tea back with us on the wagon, but Pa refreshed himself with a curious concoction called "Switchel". Switchel (also served in a mayonnaise jar) is a particularly foul-tasting libation whose main ingredient is cider vinegar. There's a little honey thrown in for good measure, but, although Pa swore by it, a swig of it would leave us boys gagging.

We didn't leave the field for lunch—that would waste too much time. Gram always knew just when the sound of adolescent stomach-grumbling would be at its peak and would arrive in the battered old Rambler station wagon with potato chips, pickles, a loaf of Wonder Bread and a batch of egg salad in—of course—a mayonnaise jar. The sun, arcing across the sky, told us our break was really just a pause and we needed to finish up lunch and get back to the job. We'd wolf down our sandwiches and Gram would putter back to the house in the Rambler.

Idyllic? I hated every minute.

My cousins lived and breathed farming, but I didn't want to waste my summer vacations bringing in hay. There were books to be read and lakes to be swum in and—most of all—old movies on T.V. to be watched. The fights my Dad and I had over me helping out on the farm were awesome. I remember him yelling once that I "read too many books!" (Translation: My son's a faggot.)

Of course, I always lost those battles and wound up on the hay wagon, broiling in the sun, hayseeds torturing me down the back of my t-shirt, sweat soaking me through and through, being nearly knocked unconscious by the errant catapulting bale and trying to keep my balance as the wagon bounced over the uneven fields. All the while knowing that there was a Norma Shearer picture on the Million Dollar Movie that would probably never be shown again!

Boy, was I a stooge.

Looking back now, I think my protestations were an essential part of the experience; maybe if I had gone along willingly the memories wouldn't be as strong, the remembered sensations not nearly as vivid. By hating every moment, I experienced every moment.

I don't picture those days in the tans and sepias of old photos. No, I see the late 1960s in the super-saturated hues of 8mm Kodachrome home movies. The sweet corn presented proudly to the camera at the picnic after finishing in the field is lemony and lush. The scarf covering the pink rollers in my aunt's hair is turquoise and diaphanous. The picture is a little blurry and the action is sped up just a little, like we're all rushing to fit as much fun as we can into our too-brief summer vacation.

I don't think Dad was right that I read too much. But, I'm dearly glad I always lost the battle and got to spend a few hot July days bouncing along on the back of an old hay wagon.

ALL WE OWE IOWA

Well, the way Randy tells it, he had just picked up his mail and there among the bills was an envelope addressed to him from his grandfather. Seems Grandpa would give each of the grandkids a check for $250 when they got married. All the other cousins had gotten their loot by this point but Randy was still unmarried. Who can say what got into the old man, but he decided to send Randy his check in spite of him still being a bachelor.

"How do you like that?" Randy said to Allen as they drove down the street in Allen's red convertible. The thing is, Randy didn't exactly consider himself "unmarried." He and Allen had been together just a short time, but it felt like The Real Thing. So they went right to the bank where Randy cashed the check and handed $125 to Allen.

"And I took it," said Allen. "And I spent it. And I haven't stopped spending since."

That check from Randy's grandfather arrived in 1973 and, according to Randy, that's when they were married. As far as the state of Iowa is concerned, however, Randy Van Syoc and Allen Coit Ransome are newlyweds who were legally married on August 26, 2009.

Randy and Allen have been my friends for just a few short years but we're as close as family. Our mutual friend Jeanine and I were the witnesses who signed the marriage license. But when their friend Ken, who officiated at the ceremony, asked who would stand for these two people, the entire crowd yelled, "We do!" and leapt to their feet.

The ceremony took place on a boat that launched onto the Mississippi from Dubuque and in the middle of the ceremony, in addition to heckling the minister, Allen instructed the captain to veer a little away from the Illinois side and further into Iowa waters *just to make sure* the marriage was legal.

All the trapping were there: the open bar; the cheese platters, the bacon-wrapped shrimp; the relatives meeting out-of-town friends for the first time. The usual. The atmosphere , though, was anything but; it felt historic and long, long overdue. Allen told me earlier in the day that he had been lying awake a few nights before the ceremony trying to come up with some appropriate vows.

"And I started to get really mad. '*Vows*?' What was left for me to promise? I realized after all these years that I had been cheated out of the chance to make vows as a young man when romance and love are fresh and making promises like that really means something."

Both of The Boys (as everyone calls them) injected a little politics into their vows but overall their words were touching and heartfelt. All the guests were in tears. And in a moment that was so over the top it wouldn't make it into the gooiest Lifetime movie, just as The Happy Couple exchanged rings a bald eagle swooped majestically down from the sky and made a U-turn past the bow of the boat before soaring back up above the water.

After the ceremony and the hugs and the kisses and the laughter and the tears we all took the stairs to the upper deck. I stood in back of the boat looking out at the endless Mississip' and couldn't help thinking that, while it may have taken Allen and Randy thirty-six years to prove it, the world, and Old Man River are not, I say *they are not*, just rollin' along.

MY HUCKLEBERRY FRIENDS

I had one of those Proustian sense memory moments at the gym this morning. As I rounded the 27-minute mark on the treadmill my iPod started playing the Sarah Vaughan swing waltz version of Henry Mancini's "Moon River," in which "Sassy" stretches out "moon" over 12—count 'em—12 syllables. As the music played I experienced a cinematic dissolve back to 1994, shortly after Henry Mancini had died. I was an ardent fan and had been saddened to learn of his death. As a tribute my husband Bruce and I decided to throw a Henry Mancini Memorial Cocktail Party. It was Pride Week and the weather was fine. We knew there would be competing events on the weekend so we called the party for 6-9 PM on Wednesday evening and asked that our guests come dressed as characters from "Breakfast at Tiffany's", the original source of "Moon River", one of my favorite songs.

I made a 90-minute Mancini compilation tape that would play over and over on the auto-reverse deck in our living room. Bruce and I felt very sophisticated as we went to the restaurant supply store in the neighborhood to stock up on cheap stemware for the event; Mancini's music was the essence of "cool" and we intended to have our soirée live up to his swinging tunes by offering nothing but martinis.

Bruce wore his all-purpose red satin tux jacket for the party while I, sporting an orange flattop at the time, made a stunning Rusty Trawler in my white dinner jacket and black sunglasses with the lenses popped out. When our guests started to arrive we were pleased to find that everyone had gotten into the spirit of things and dressed for the occasion. A beret here, a taffeta party dress there, and much chunky costume jewelry on both sexes. We had dueling Holly Golightlys at one point but fortunately no blood was spilled. Jeffrey and Tim showed up in vintage suits and were chastised for their usual lateness by Kyle who brandished a martini in one of her gloved hands and a long cigarette holder in the other. Ann Magnuson was out of town and sent her brother, Bobby, as proxy. Even Steve Brown, the cynic's cynic, only mentioned once or twice how ridiculous we all were. Bruce trolled the room with a pitcher of vodka while I followed behind armed with an eyedropper of vermouth. Between us our guests never wanted for their dry, extra-dry or parched martinis.

The Stolichnaya flowed freely, the conversation increased steadily in both volume and hilarity and above it all Henry Mancini looked down approvingly from the framed studio publicity shot I had found in a junk store on 2nd Avenue. I cupped my hand to Bruce's ear so he could hear me over the "Peter Gunn Theme" that blared from the speakers. "We did it, honey; this *is* the party from 'Breakfast at Tiffany's'." Bruce had to agree as he looked around the room at our wonderful friends drinking and laughing and Twisting to the music.

At almost 9 o'clock on the dot in a moment of serendipity the tape reversed itself in the cassette deck and began to play the introduction to "Moon River." As the plaintive harmonica started on the opening notes of the melody everyone in the room spontaneously chose partners and began to slow dance. With Bobby Magnuson in my arms I floated past our living room window and looked out to see the towers of the World Trade Center silhouetted against the pink-and-orange sunset. What a perfect world, I thought to myself.

But that evening in June, 1994 was only a brief respite from a world that was far from perfect. The AIDS crisis was in full swing and many of our friends—including several at our party—were beginning to show symptoms of the disease. The more effective drug cocktails were still more than a year away and the sense of fear was almost inescapable. But we managed to escape it that night as, dressed in our silly party clothes, we said goodbye and farewell to Henry Mancini.

As I rode the treadmill this morning I thought back to that summer evening with a warm nostalgia that only the passage of a dozen years has made possible. Almost half the guests at our party had died by the end of the decade and the memory of them waltzing to "Moon River" makes me smile. But as I watch Tim and Jeffrey arguing over which of them will lead I see them start to disappear even as they waltz, leaving too soon just as they arrived late. Steve Brown sitting in the big chair, obstinately refusing to dance, dematerializes as he rolls his eyes in my direction. Suddenly I find myself dancing alone as Bobby Magnuson evaporates from my arms. And when I look across the room at Bruce, laughing as he steps on Kyle's toes yet again, he simply fades away along with the final bars of the song..

So many friends gone. But with Henry Mancini's help they occasionally do unexpectedly reappear. Why, there they are now, just waitin' 'round the bend for Moon River and me.

" . . . SO THAT WE MAY BRING YOU . . . "

There was a time when entire families gathered in the soft glow of the cathode ray of a console television, hushing one another, as an announcer, in sober, stentorian tones, proclaimed, *"Our regularly scheduled program will not be seen this evening so that we may bring you a Special Presentation in Living Color."*

Of course, that brief announcement sometimes spelled disaster: The Watergate Hearings were broadcast from May through July, 1973, uncomfortably overlapping summer vacation, a span of time I had allocated to uninterrupted TV viewing.

Suffice to say that the episodes of "The Match Game" that weren't obliterated by summer sunspots were more often than not trammeled by Sam Ervin & Co. (I never watched the hearings unless John Dean was testifying—I found him strangely sexy and, even as a 12-year-old homo, I appreciated the steely resolve his wife exuded as she sat behind him in her tailored suits and bleached hair pulled tightly into a bun.)

But, fortunately, a preempted program usually brought something truly special in its place. "Peter Pan" and "The Wizard of Oz" come to mind. Our entire extended family would traipse to my grandmother's, as she possessed the only color television set in the clan.

It seems that there were more preemptions during the holidays than at any other time of the year as the networks hauled out their variety shows and "spectaculars" as early Christmas gifts to the nation.

My family devoured them all. Halfway through "Christmas With Ray Conniff and the Singers" my mother announced she was convinced that they were just mouthing along to the album. All four of us kids stampeded out of the living room and returned with the portable record player. After making sure the needle was flipped from 78 to LP we discovered that Mom was right: our scratchy copy of "Christmas With Ray Conniff and the Singers" synched up perfectly with the voices on T.V.

Was this a good thing or not? Were the people on television sipping cocoa around a roaring fire displaying uncanny abilities or were we at home getting gypped? For that matter, were these photogenic men and women members of The Ray

Conniff Singers at all? Mom had unwittingly opened a can of worms with her revelation and planted the seeds of skepticism in a young mind.

Which only meant she had an even harder time trying to explain why Katie from "My Three Sons" was on "The King Family Christmas Special." Did Robbie Douglas know his wife was leading this parallel life, that she had all these blond relatives and that she *sang*? And, most of all, what about their triplets? From my own experience I knew that fathers had little, if anything, to do with raising a family, so, who was watching all those kids? Try as I might, I couldn't imagine Beverly Garland changing a diaper. My anxiety kept me from being able to fully enjoy the show.

Most Holiday Spectaculars followed this basic variety show format, but, one night in 1964, a truly special Special premiered on NBC; "Rudolph, the Red-Nosed Reindeer", presented in something called "Animagic" was shown for the first time in what would become an uninterrupted 40-year run. Here was a holiday special for the *whole* family. Even little gay boys found something in it for them; something that only grew richer and more meaningful with the passing years. *We* understood exactly what Rudolph went through; who didn't endure that kind of taunting from the other kids at school? But, it wasn't Rudolph with whom budding queers most closely identified, for there among the elves—in a *principal role*—was one outright, glorious queen.

Consider this dialogue from the choir practice scene in original script:

FOREMAN
(furious)
That sounded terrible. What's wrong with you guys? The tenor section was weak!!

AN ELF
Wasn't our fault, boss. Hermey didn't show up.

FOREMAN
WHAT!! Where is that little. . .
(Stops himself.)

I think we all know what the Foreman intended to say.

Hermey the Gay Dentist Elf was unapologetically fabulous. (And let's get this straight; it's *Hermey*, not Herbie.) He, alone, stood out from his oafish co-workers. In the scene above, when the Foreman was asking his whereabouts, Hermey had all the dolls in the workshop lined up working on their teeth, but he could have just as easily been perfecting that *swoosh* of blond hair that could only have been achieved with a 2000-watt hand dryer and a round brush. With his sense of style and insouciant wit, Hermey was the Carson Kressley of his day.

I venture to guess Hermey wasn't all that disappointed climbing out the workshop window, leaving behind the only home he knew for the Big Wide World, uncertain as it was. After all, potential fame, fortune and a Park Avenue practice awaited him.

When Hermey and Rudolph arrive on the Island of Misfit Toys they find the place we've all been longing for: everyone fits in precisely because they're *all* misfits. It's the Greenwich Village of the North Pole. (And, by the way, if you've been wondering all these years what's wrong with the little girl dolly, well, there's *nothing* wrong with her; my guess is she's just a Misfit Hag who gets her kicks hanging around square-wheeled locomotives because it makes her feel superior.)

It seemed like such a perfect little world that, to me, it made no sense to leave. I imagined the toys sitting around the skating rink, frozen cocktails in hand, marveling at how wonderful it is to be unique. (Not to mention that Lion King Daddy with the deep voice. *Grrrr*, indeed.)

But, leaving the island was what the toys wanted, and getting back home was what Rudolph wanted and—all thanks to Hermey the Gay Elf—that's exactly what they got. Yup, The Homo saved the day by extracting the tooth that made the Snowmonster so Abominable. True, he had to fall over a cliff in the process, but here was one pre-Stonewall drama that didn't require that the homosexual take his own life or suffer a tragic death. Oh, and he survived the precipitous plunge just fine, thanks. ("That's the thing about Bumbles—Bumbles *bounce!*")

In no small way I feel we all owe Hermey a debt of gratitude. He matter-of-factly showed us all that it's not only alright to be a fey, stylish individual, standing out from a bunch of brutish conformists, following an unlikely life-path, but that by doing so we might even help save Christmas.

SHOPLIFTING FIRE

The phone rang around two A.M. on a beautiful summer night. The man on the other end of the phone asked if I could come to the Towers at the Waldorf-Astoria on a job. I had already seen a client earlier that evening, but I was still wide awake, so I agreed to take a trip to the East Side. He said he was in the guest room to Suite 1612 (*Guest room?* Hotel rooms have guest rooms?) and that I had to be extremely quiet. The very rich *are* different from you and me.

As my cab sped through Rockefeller Center I noticed that the statue of Prometheus, which usually sits in the fountain of the skating rink, had been raised up onto the sidewalk in front of 30 Rockefeller Plaza. I recalled reading in the paper about some work being done on the fountain that necessitated the temporary removal of the golden statue. It was the first time since the 1930s that it had been out of its usual location and it seemed a little embarrassed to be loafing on the pavement.

Alighting from the taxi, I paid my fare and headed into the side entrance of the hotel. Since I was going to the Towers, I walked across the lobby toward the elevators designated specifically for that private area of the Waldorf. Still manned by an operator, these cabs are of the same vermillion as those in the main lobby, but they're a bit smaller, more intimate.

As the operator held the door for me, I stepped in to find another passenger already there. A lovely young woman, beautifully dressed with long, straight black hair, looked demurely down at her feet.

"Floors, please?" I gave mine as sixteen, the young woman as four below that. Save for the humming of the lift cables, we ascended in silence until we landed at twelve. The woman stepped out of the car and looked uncertainly both ways down the corridor before walking to the right. The elevator door closed and the car started to rise once more. The operator glanced quickly in my direction. "Hooker," he snorted. Momentarily stunned at his perception I paused before replying, "Oh, the girl! How can you tell?" "I can just tell," he answered. A barely audible "Hmmm..." was the best that I could muster in response.

"Sixteen. Watch your step, sir." I nodded to the man, who added, "Have a good night, sir." Unsure of which direction my destination lay, but aware that the elevator man was watching me, I strode purposefully down the hallway to the left. Only when I heard the door glide shut behind me did I take the opportunity to look at the numbers on the room doors and discover that I was headed in the right direction.

I got to Suite 1612 and, sure enough, just below the brass number plate was another that read "Guest room" with an arrow pointing to the left. I rounded the corner, tapped gently on the door and heard footsteps approach on the other side. The peephole went dark for a moment and then the door swung open. Standing there was a man in his mid-to-late 40s clad in just a towel wrapped around his waist. He was quite handsome, in a Burt Bacharach, Malibu-surfer-boy-gone-to-seed kind of way. I liked him instantly.

I walked past him into the room and turned to face him as he shut the door. I smiled, and as I drew in my breath to say hello, he clapped his hand over my mouth. Backing me across the room, I lost my balance when we reached the bed and we fell onto it, him on top of me, with his hand still tight across my mouth. "You have to be quiet" he whispered as his blue eyes bore into mine. I nodded yes. "You can't make a sound," he said as he slowly removed his hand and brushed his fingers gently across my face. I looked at him for a moment and then silently mouthed, "Why not?"

"Because my wife and her parents are in the main suite."

What was already a very sexy moment instantly became even more erotic. A smile spread across my face and I pulled his ear down next to my mouth. "You're nuts," I whispered. He looked at me and shrugged. I put my hand behind his neck and pulled him towards me and started to kiss him. As we kissed he started to unbutton my shirt, running his hand over my chest and pinching my nipples, which caused me to moan. He abruptly raised himself up on his hands and gave me a look that said, "What did I tell you?" I nodded reassuringly and rolled him over so I was now on top. I slowly kissed my way down his body and undid the towel from around his waist. As I put his hard dick in my mouth he let out a small sound. We looked at each other for a split second and then both laughed silently. I stood up and finished undressing as he sat up on the end of the bed and started caressing my legs and ass. I leaned over to kiss him again and we lay back down on the bed.

In a bit I found myself lying on my back with him over me as he jerked himself off to a climax. He was kissing me when he came, and I could feel the muscles in his mouth relax just as the rest of his body tensed and he shot his load on my stomach and chest. He sighed deeply and then collapsed on the bed next to me. He scooped his cum off my body and used it to jack me off. I lay there, looking into his eyes and, just as I was about to cum, he gently put his hand over my mouth (which drove me crazy) causing me to have an intense, silent orgasm.

As we lay there looking up at the ceiling, I could feel him turn to face me. I raised up on one elbow and whispered into his ear, "Come for a walk with me. I want to show you something." To my surprise he nodded yes.

We dressed in silence and he paid me, throwing in a $100 tip. Riding down to the lobby in the elevator, the operator wore a quizzical expression but kept his thoughts to himself. As we spun through the revolving doors onto a nearly deserted Park Avenue I turned to my new friend and said, "What the hell was going on up there?!"

He explained that he and his wife and her parents had all been out to dinner that night and had drunk a lot of wine. That's why he was confident they wouldn't be bursting through the connecting door from the suite. They were all flying back to Los Angeles in the morning.

"What time does your plane leave?"

"Whenever we want it to."

Oh, I see.

As we headed—mostly in silence—over to Rockefeller Center I explained that he was going to see a once-in-a-lifetime sight. I pointed out various architectural and cultural landmarks on the way and, as we walked down the Channel gardens (so-called because the England building lies on one side of them and the France building on the other) I nudged his shoulder with my own and said, "Y'know, you johns aren't supposed to be so sexy." Without missing a beat he responded, "Yeah? Well, you hookers aren't supposed to be so smart." I chuckled and put my hand on the back of his neck, giving it a little squeeze.

We stood there on the street, gazing up at Prometheus, his hand outstretched, forever brandishing the fire he stole from the gods. My focus slowly traveled to the man standing next to me, his profile silhouetted by the lights of the skating rink, and I thought to myself that I had done a little flame-stealing of my own that night. I suppose the sordid details of my heist brought it closer to the level of a petty theft, but there was definitely fire involved.

We said goodnight and he got into a cab. I decided to walk home and headed west just as the morning sky was fading from silver to rose.

I never saw or heard from the guest in the guest room again, so I don't know if what he told me about who slept on the other side of that door was the truth or not.

But I really don't care.

VINO E CUCINA

The beaded curtain clicked pleasantly behind me as I entered the restaurant. The streets outside were dusty and hot, the air humid and still; but here, under the vaulted ceiling, it was cool. A small table against the wall held an old plastic radio whose cord was plugged into an outlet in the ceiling. Next to the radio sat a small fan whirring silently as the breeze it created blew ribbons attached to the blade housing. The radio played Italian songs and the tunes were obscured by static whenever the fan reached a certain place in its sweep.

The room was clean, if spare. Four or five tables sat evenly spaced on the tiled floor, each laid with a blue checked cloth with a dark blue border and, over that, a sheet of heavy plastic. A capped bottle of water and a tall glass filled with packaged breadsticks sat on each table, along with two single-ply paper napkins folded into triangles. Mismatched chairs were pushed neatly underneath.

As my eyes adjusted to the dark, I saw that five of the tables were empty. At the sixth sat an old lady dressed in black, her white hair tied in a tight bun and a pair of gloves resting on the table next to a black purse. Before her was a plate of food and a half-liter of wine. I nodded to her as I sat the table nearest the door, but she just sneered in response.

The owner emerged from the kitchen and greeted me in Italian. Neither of us spoke the other's language, so he took me by the elbow to a table placed just outside the kitchen door. Here the dishes of the house were proudly displayed. I attempted to explain that I didn't eat meat, but when he insisted—in English—that his pork chops were as beautiful as children, I agreed to try them.

The old lady watched me as I ate and read my book. I found it difficult to concentrate under her gimlet eye and raised my glass to her as I took a sip.

Again she sneered.

I finished my meal and paid the bill, thinking this would be a good place to come back to tomorrow. It was just across the Arno from the Vatican and near all the sights I wanted to see and explore. And the pork chops were as beautiful as children.

As I passed the old lady's table I nodded to her and, as I bent my head toward her, saw that what had appeared to be a sneer was actually a cleft palate; a "harelip." I hurried out of the restaurant, uncomfortable and embarrassed.

To earn a living after my grandfather died, my grandmother ran what was essentially a private nursing home. She "took in ladies," as she called it.

One of Gram's ladies was an old, mean woman with a cleft palate. My sisters and I were frightened of her when we visited and would avoid as much as possible having to speak to her. When this woman was well into her seventies someone, somehow, paid for her to have corrective surgery. She returned home to my grandmother's a smiling, sweet old lady.

I don't know if her countenance really improved with her appearance or if her deformity had disguised what had been a sunny nature all along, but we were no longer frightened of her.

When I returned to the café the following day I decided to assume the old lady's sneer was her way of returning my smile when I greeted her with a "buon giorno" as I passed her table.

The third day, as I approached the restaurant, I saw her standing just outside the door, looking expectantly down the street in the opposite direction. She saw me as she turned and hurried inside to her table. I passed through the beaded curtain and stopped at her table to wish her good day. The old lady still didn't respond to my greetings, but I was no longer afraid of her. I sat at a table and enjoyed a scallopini that was as beautiful as a child.

I saw no reason to alter my routine on my final day in Rome. As I stepped into the café I heard not only the radio that sat on the little table against the wall, but three chattering voices as well.

My friend had company; two old ladies with hair just as white and dresses just as black as her own. Their conversation stopped abruptly as I entered the restaurant. I walked directly over to their table, made a little bow, and said, "Buon giorno, Signora."

"Buon giorno," she replied, as her old lady friend looked first at me and then at her.

Two years later, on my next visit to Italy, I managed to find the little café with the vaulted ceiling in the warren of streets across the Tiber from The Vatican. It had gone out of business and was vacant. I cupped my hands and put my face up to the glass in the door. I'd like to say I saw a table with a pair of white gloves lying neatly on the faded cloth. But the room was empty.

All that was left was the sign above the door and a memory of pork chops as beautiful as children.

OYSTERS, ROCKEFELLER?

"Sure, I'd love to go. But, it's pricey, y'know? Aren't you always broke?"

Such was the response from my cousin Frannie when I asked if she'd like to join me for oysters and martinis at The Oyster Bar in Grand Central Terminal. I've been treating myself to the occasional visit to that elegant subterranean shoal a level and a half below 42nd Street for more than fifteen years now. And, yes, it *is* expensive, but it's money well spent. I see nothing wrong with such an extravagance every six or eight months.

Besides, I feel slightly proprietary of the place as several major scenes in my un-produced screenplay are set there.

Since Bruce died I usually sit at the counter by myself; a dozen oysters chilling patiently on the chipped ice spread out in a wide, white dish on the bar in front of me as I take in the hubbub of the place. But, I hadn't seen Frannie (Bruce was *her* cousin, after all) in quite a while and I knew her company would be as glittery as the terra cotta tiles that line the walls and ceiling of this landmark restaurant. Our family is convinced Alison Janney based her character of C. J. Craig on "The West

Wing" on Frannie, so not only is time spent with her time to be treasured, but one has to stay on one's toes, as well. (It seems cousin-bating is her favorite sport.)

What better spot than The Oyster Bar to debate current events and lob *bon mots* back and forth at each other, defending our points with the parry and thrust of a tooth-picked olive?

I arrived at Grand Central a few minutes early, so, I made my entrance down the escalator form the Pan Am Building, taking in the wide sweep of the main waiting room—surely on of the grandest spaces in New York, if not all of America. The constellations painted on the ceiling above shone happily down on the rush-hour travelers and the piped-in holiday music gave the moment a particularly festive feeling. From up above on the moving stairway the floor of the station resembled an undulating ant farm. And, like a squadron of ants, upon closer inspection there was perfect method to the madness; everyone seemed to know exactly where they were headed and at the precise tempo they needed to move to make their trains, to meet their partners, to shortcut from Lexington to Vanderbilt Avenues on this cold night with the mercury fast approaching freezing.

In the brief time I stood watching, I saw a surprising number of faces with furrowed brows that melted into wide smiles that were then met by a second set of lips in a warm kiss. From this I gathered there were more than a few telephone conversations across Manhattan earlier in the day that had ended with, "So, I'll meet you under the clock."

My own conversation with Frannie had ended, "So, I'll meet you outside the restaurant," which is why I walked down the marble stairs and waited in front of The Oyster Bar opposite Track 109. Minutes later I performed my own version of the brow/smile/kiss metamorphosis as Frannie walked up to me and wrapped me in her arms.

"Hey, cuz," (her usual greeting,) "I'm so glad you asked me to come tonight. Let's go in—I want a drink."

Each time I walk into The Oyster Bar my focus involuntarily travels up and around the vaulted ceilings. Created in 1913 the ceiling is a landmark unto itself. The lines of the arches lead one's eyes to the tables covered with read-and-white checked cloths in the restaurant area, then to the serpentine lunch counter covered in spotless white Formica. Finally, after optically traversing the ceiling, one's gaze comes to rest on the Oyster Bar proper; a long, tile-faced counter set in front of the shucking station.

This is where I sit.

We walked across the room to the bar feeling impossibly hip. A hipness of an accessible variety, though—the room suggests the Hi-Los more than it does Lambert, Hendricks and Ross. It's more Greenwich, Connecticut then Greenwich Village.

We sat in the middle of the bar, a spot that allows an oyster eater to literally watch the world go by: behind the shucking station a large, multi-paned, gothic-arched window looks out onto the ramp leading from the main concourse to the lower level of the station. Commuters paraded nonstop for our perusal and we had fun reading way too much symbolism into their strides.

Frannie and I hadn't seen each other in quite some time, so we both had a lot to tell. Assuring me that "as long as I'm happy doing porn," it's fine with her, (the, "I'll sit in the dark," was implied,) she continued, "besides, every family needs a black sheep." Then I made her cry by relating some of the wonderful e-mails I've received from total strangers. By the end of our visit she was proclaiming (in the full volume of a 2-martini voice), "I can't believe you're saying 'porn star' out loud at The Oyster Bar!"

Between trying to talk over each other to bring the other up to speed on our respective lives, we managed to order a dozen oysters from Carlos, the counter man. We opted for six Kumamotos *(like butter!)* and the other half-dozen at the discretion of the shucker.

Along with the large platter of oysters on ice, a smaller white plate is set on the counter with a couple of little pleated paper soufflé cups. These contain the two condiments for the bivalve feast: in one is to be found ketchup for cocktail sauce, (at The Oyster bar you mix your own with the horseradish on the counter,) and in the other, *sauce mignonette*. I prefer the latter, because it's vinegary like me. Not much more than wine vinegar and shallots, really, it lays a piquant blossom of flavor onto the oyster that causes a most pleasant burning sensation upon swallowing (after *just one bite* of the oyster to taste it.)

All told, it required a dozen and a half (and two martinis each) to fill in the blanks on what we had each been up to since we last spent any time together, but, by that time, Frannie and I both had to get going. We paid the check (which was, in fact, glamorously expensive) and, headed up the ramp to the main floor.

Stepping through the terminal doors out onto 42nd Street we were hit by a blast of frigid air. Looking eastward for a cab my eye was caught by the huge clock looming above the terminal, watched over by winged Mercury.

"Hey, Frannie," I said, "this is exactly where a scene from my movie takes place."

"So, are you gonna tell me what happens in it or are you just going to stand there while I freeze to death?

"Well, these two guys meet at a cocktail party and they walk down Park Avenue together on a beautiful summer evening. . . "

DISSOLVE TO. . .

> JOE and WILLIAM are now stopped on 42nd Street in front of Grand Central.

> JOE
> (indicating the clock high above the terminal)
> That clock is one of my favorite things in New York.

> WILLIAM
> Why's that?

> JOE
> Well, it's beautiful, obviously, and monumental. But, I just love thinking about everything that it's seen; all the things that have gone on underneath it. Husbands racing to catch their trains home. . . women

coming into town for a show. Kids like me coming in from the boondocks, hoping to make a success in the big city... Soldiers saying goodbye to their girlfriends on their way to war, not knowing if they'll come back... children growing up and then growing old; murders; births, probably; love, hate; everything that could possibly happen in the life of a city. And ol' Mercury just sits up there observing it all. Not passing judgment on anyone—not even if they're late for a train. It's like... it's like he's the custodian of human events. Collecting them all and using them to keep the springs wound in the clock of life.

WILLIAM looks at JOE.

WILLIAM

You mean maybe even us meeting tonight?

JOE

Oh, yeah, I think so. For sure.

After sharing oysters with Frannie, I'd have to say Joe is right: there are a whole lot of springs in that clock. And some of them are pretty tightly-wound. But once in a while—just once in a while, mind you—you find yourself with a perfect pearl.

SO, THIS GUY CHECKS IN TO A HOSPITAL

"Does anyone know a ten-letter word for 'dazzling'?"

It was the only clue left in the puzzle, which was surprising, considering the company that night. I was met with a chorus of "no" and "we gave up on that one," so I tossed the paper down on the table and looked around the room.

Pretty much everybody was there and, to be honest, we were all feeling a little dopey. It was the end of a long day at the end of a long couple of weeks and exhaustion had devolved to giddiness. Somehow the talk had turned to cocktails and we all started reeling off our favorites. Frannie's was a martini with a twist and Bruce's sister preferred wine to hard liquor. Bruce's mom said if she had to pick something it would be champagne. I was in Frannie's court, although I usually garnish my martinis with an olive.

Then Bruce's Aunt mentioned Campari. A visible shudder went around the room like a wave at the playoffs. I had tried that bottled Campari-and-Soda thing a couple of times when Bruce and I were in Italy, but just hadn't been able to acquire a taste for the bitter ruby-red aperitif. Tonight there was an "ycch" from this part of the room and a "no thanks" from over there, but there were no takers on Campari as a favorite.

Bruce's aunt sat placidly on the couch, one leg crossing the other so that the two were absolutely vertical, her Mona Lisa smile perfectly conveying her benign contempt for the uninitiated among us.

"Well, you've obviously never had a Negroni," was her response.

We all admitted that was true.

Bruce's uncle came into the waiting room and picked up the newspaper.

"Does anyone know . . . "

"I'm talking," scolded Shelley, as her husband sat with the *Times* resting on one knee. "A Negroni is Campari, sweet vermouth and vodka. It's a wonderful cocktail."

This endorsement, coming from someone who puts pepper on her oatmeal, left me dubious, but I promised I'd try one at dinner.

"So, what's a ten-letter word. . . "

"We don't know!" answered the group in unison. "If we knew we would have filled it in," said Bruce's sister.

"C'mon, dinner!" announced Bruce's dad. I'm hungry.

As well stood up to leave Frannie said she'd just wait here.

"But you need to eat something."

"Just bring me back something," she said. "Anything, I don't care," she said to pre-empt a discussion.

"I'll stay and keep you company," I said as everyone was putting on their coats.

"But your Negroni," said Bruce's aunt. "I know, I'll get it to go."

"You can't get liquor to go," chastised Bruce's dad.

"*She* can," answered Bruce's uncle.

The whole group left for dinner, their mission of returning with a Negroni turning the excursion into an adventure, not just an excuse to eat.

And so, as the door swung silently closed Frannie and I found ourselves alone in the visitors' waiting room of the I.C.U. on the last night of Bruce's life. Visiting hours had long since ended, but the staff had pretty much given us the run of the place. Matters were clearly reaching a conclusion and I suppose they figured there was no harm.

"Hey, Cuz, why don't you lie down over here?" I crossed the room and sprawled out on the blue vinyl-covered couch, resting my head in Frannie's lap. Her nails felt good as she gently scratched my scalp and my mind started replaying the previous few days as I stared at the drop ceiling overhead. Considering the life-and-death seriousness of the situation, there had been an awful lot of laughter in that brightly-lit room on upper 5th Avenue.

A week earlier, shortly after Bruce had checked in, a Scrabble game was underway in the waiting room. Bruce's Mom gave a sly little smile and started to place her tiles on the board, announcing that, including the double-word bonus, she had 42 points. We watched in anticipation as she spelled out J-E-W-B-O-Y.

No way! It's not really a word and, if it were, it would be hyphenated, we challenged. Besides, you can't leave that word lying around on a Scrabble board at Mt. Sinai! After startling several arriving visitors with "Jew boy should be hyphenated, right?" we finally acquiesced and granted Bruce's Mom her 42 points.

A couple of days later his dad and I were talking in the waiting room. I had my feet up on the coffee table that was filled with outdated magazines and somehow mentioned I had been the organist and choir director in my church all during high school. "Wait a minute," he said, cutting me off in a melodramatic stop-the-presses manner. "You mean you're not Jewish?" As if this fact was somehow going to be a problem at this point.

As things became more and more grim we realized we needed to make some decisions. Everyone in the family was fine with my wish to have Bruce cremated, but they weren't sure how his Mom would feel about it. I worked it so the two of us were alone in the waiting room and, screwing up my courage, explained to her that, shortly after we met, Bruce and I had gone to their house by the ocean in Rhode Island. We took a bottle of champagne to the beach on a cold, gray December day and talked and talked. It's when we knew we were in love. I told her I wanted him cremated so, at some point in the future, our ashes could be scattered together on that beach.

"I just want to know one thing," she said, looking at me exactly like a protective mother would. "Did you guys buy the champagne yourselves or did you take it out of my pantry?" Laughing, I jumped out of my seat and crossed the room to hug her.

"What is it, cuz?"

Frannie's question brought me back to the present. I guess I must have been sniffling a little; she wiped a tear from underneath my eye as my head lay in her lap.

"When this is all over I just hope, well, I still want to be part of the family."

Frannie's hand grabbed a clump of my hair and she gave it a gentle tug. "Huh! You're not getting rid of us that easy!"

I sat upright and turned to face her.

"That easy?!"

We stared at each other long enough for the total absurdity of what she had said sunk in and then we simultaneously burst out laughing. We were in the throws of hilarity when the door opened and the group came back in from dinner. Bruce's aunt led the way flourishing a cardboard coffee cup in each hand.

"One martini to go," she said, handing a cup to Frannie. "And one Negroni, as promised."

The cocktails made Frannie and me even giddier and caught us up with the drinking that had gone on at dinner, all of which served to increase the volume of our conversation significantly. When the nurse came in to ask us all to hold it down a little, we decided we should probably call it a night. We knew they'd call us if anything dramatic happened during the night.

And it did. They called several hours later and we all made our way back to the hospital. Not a heck of a lot of laughter during that visit, as I recall.

I still feel my spirits dip every year as April 18 approaches. But enough time has passed so that my strongest memory of that night involves an unfinished crossword puzzle, a lot of laugher and a Negroni in a cardboard cup.

How to make the perfect Negroni: 1 ounce each Campari, sweet vermouth and vodka. Stir with ice and pour into a cardboard to-go coffee cup. Serve under fluorescent lights and garnish with a lemon twist and laughter.

WINDS FROM THE SOUTH

Two millennia ago the Roman elite went by barge across the Bay of Naples to one of the most beautiful islands in the world, a journey that took most of the day. In the final decade of the 20th century, I found myself making the same trip, but I traveled *above* the surface of the water in a hydrofoil and I would arrive less than an hour after pushing off from the pier in *Napoli*. My reason for going to Capri, however, was very different from that of the Caesars: they went to shed their cares. I was going to leave some of my late husband's ashes.

I say "husband" because, long before the issue of same-sex marriage entered the national debate, there was really no other word to define the relationship Bruce and I shared. It was intimate and lovely. We had private jokes that only we understood; we fought about sex and money, something understood by *every* married couple.

Bruce had died from AIDS five months before, which meant we never got to take the trip to southern Italy that was to be our next vacation. So I decided to go alone.

We had traveled extensively, and I had wanted to share with him this wonderful, lemony island, which had counted among its guests not just the Caesars but such diverse personalities as Somerset Maugham and Clark Gable. And Bruce would be able to practice his (very) limited Italian. As expressive and animated as he was, he could never quite wrap his mouth around "*grazie.*" He would veer from "*gracias*" to "*graziass,*" never landing on the correct pronunciation, until he finally settled on an all-purpose "*grah...,*" letting the recipient of his thanks fill in the rest mentally. The waiters generally understood what he meant by "*grah...*", and he would beam like a little boy at his new-found ability. (He did, once, manage to form the word correctly and with a perfect Italian accent. The hotel-keep in Madrid was mightily impressed.)

On this trip I stayed at the Hotel Caesar Augustus which, in 1996, was still an elegant but slightly dilapidated relic of the halcyon days before the war. Its ochre stucco arches opened onto a terrace that boasted a spectacular—if vertiginous—view. The azure sea lay a dizzying 1,000 feet below, and spotlights mounted on the cliff just beneath the terrace illuminated the hotel's clean art-deco lines.

I decided I would toss Bruce's ashes off that terrace on the final night of my stay, which I thought would be a fitting end to my trip.

For three days I moped around Capri. One evening I dined in an empty restaurant which the night before had hummed with a chorus of German and English voices. I asked where everyone had gone and was told, "But, it is the Scirocco!" Like an actor making a well-rehearsed entrance, the fabled wind from North Africa had arrived perfectly on schedule bringing with it a faint hint of spice and mystery as well as a never-ceasing breeze. It rose and fell in intensity, but never, ever stopped.

On my last night there I had dinner and drank too much wine. As I wandered back to the hotel, I tried to think of anything but the task ahead.

In the months since Bruce died, I had found myself completely at the mercy of my emotions, so I wasn't sure how this scene would play out. When the last of Bruce's ashes had drifted down to the sea, would I throw myself after them? Or would I collapse like a puddle onto the terra cotta tiles and have to be helped to my room as the hotel staff whispered about "the sad, sad *Americano*"?

I walked across the lobby and pushed open the heavy glass doors of the terrace. There were one or two couples leaning against the wall nearby, so I found a secluded, dimly lit spot out of their sight.

I reached inside my jacket and reluctantly took the packet out of my breast pocket. The ashes had remained—literally—close to my heart since I had boarded the Alitalia flight at JFK two weeks before. I was not terribly anxious to let them go now. The moon shone plaintively on the water, and I tried focusing on its liquid reflection to maintain my composure. As I opened the envelope and poured the ashes into my palm, I whispered a few words of love and remembrance. "Well, Bruce, I guess we made it to Capri after all," I thought. I brought my hand to my mouth and kissed the closed fingers before drawing my hand back over my head. I mustered all my strength and resolve as I threw.

And then the Scirocco seized control of the moment: a *whoosh* of air blew the ashes up and over my head. They were caught in the blazing lights below the terrace and transformed into a spray of stars. I might as well call it what it was: my husband was circling overhead in a cloud of *fairy dust*. After dancing in the air for a few moments, the ashes blew giddily away into the night.

I stood there open-mouthed, transfixed.

What made them shimmer so? Was it Bruce's silvery laugh? His sparkling smile? Most likely it was just flecks of bone and tissue. But it brought from deep inside me a sound that might best be described as the marriage of a sob and a chuckle.

And that perfectly timed gust of wind? I suspect that was Bruce laughing at my solemnity and forcing me to see the moment as something wondrous. He robbed me of a good cry that night but never has a victim submitted so gladly to a thief's demand. I wanted to cry out, "*Grah! Grah!*"

I have not been back to Capri since that night eight years ago. But, when I do I'll stand gazing out over the moonlit sea and listen for Bruce's distant laugh in the warm, faint breath of the Scirocco.

A NOTE ON SOURCES

This volume was assembled after repeated requests from readers for a compendium of my essays, which were scattered among many sources and publications. For those who are interested, the original sources are listed below.

They're Playing Our Song
The Beauty Curse
The Church of Me
Norman Rae
—*Unzipped Magazine*

Tradewinds
Did You Have View?
—Saba blog

Houses of Worship
An Empty Bowl
Little Miss Indian Giver
Him and His Shadow
Recounting the Abbotts
Cicciolina, Miss America and Me
Come Out, Come Out, Wherever You Are
The House Painter

Panhandle Manhandle
Rattlesnakes Have Been Observed
We Shall Come Rejoicing
My Huckleberry Friends
So That We May Bring You
Shoplifting Fire
Vino e Cucina
Oysters, Rockefeller?
So, This Guy Checks In To A Hospital. . .
Winds From the South
—Gus's Soapbox

Rigatoni With Sausage and Fennel
September 25, 1 A.M.
—Gus Mattox blog

The Longest Mile
All We Owe Iowa
—Tom Judson blog

A Million Men
—*Blue Magazine*

Howard, We Hardly Knew Ye
—*Equity News*

Made in the USA
Lexington, KY
22 March 2013